LEGAL FICTIONS

NCQ TITLES

Legal Fictions
Politics & Letters
On Yeats: Upon a House
Drama & Democracy
Locating Theology
Time Pieces
Critical Paranoia
On Joyce: 3 easy essays
On Eliot
Literary Conversions

Film texts

A Trip to Rome
A Short Break in Budapest
Magic in Prague
A Week in Venice
Four Days in Athens
The Last Priest of Horus
WWW: the weekend that warped the world

Play texts

Darwin: an evolutionary entertainment
Strange Meetings & Shorts

Eliotics

Forthcoming

Rubbishing Hockney & other reviews
On Collecting Walter Benjamin
Autobiography & Class Consciousness
Considering Canterbury Cathedral

Though each can be read independently,
these NCQ publications, taken together,
comprise a single hyper-text collection.

LEGAL FICTIONS

Bernard Sharratt

New Crisis Quarterly
2015

NEW CRISIS QUARTERLY

ncq@newcrisisquarterly.myzen.co.uk

First published 2015

ISBN : 978-1-910956-04-5

F*or*
Brian Simpson
Peter Fitzpatrick
& Clare Palley
who taught me to think
about law differently

CONTENTS

FOREWORD

These essays taken together offer an account of various literary works as a way of exploring and understanding some of the issues endemic to any legal system, its forms of investigation and prosecution, its often problematic principles and procedures. The essays are arranged in an order which is partly historical and partly systemic.

At times, the legal issues explored overlap into concerns perhaps more apparently germane to the philosophy of science and to the nature of reasoning itself, with implications for notions of political thought, and the possibility of rational democratic thinking. Some of these related and underlying issues are considered more directly in my *Drama and Democracy*, where the highly compressed account of Greek drama in *Raisons des textes* may one day, I hope, be expanded into a short book on Greek tragedy.

For now, this book simply reprints the *Legal Fictions* section of my *Reading Relations* , published in.1982, but out of print since the publisher, Harvester, was incorporated into some larger conglomerate. In its prevous incarnation this series of compressed exercises was part of an rather elaborate overall formal structure, basically counterposing explorations of various ideological domains, especially law, education, and religion, against an historical analysis of the ongoing political impasses of the labour movement. What I had intended to construct was an enactment of what Lucien Goldmann termed a 'tragic vision', consitutued at one level by an apparent incompatibility between two alternative approaches to socialist thinking, but generated most basically by a real and peristent stalemate or impasse in socialist strategy.

The mock exam format, retained form that formal arrangement, provides a flexible schema for exploring specific legal procedures and roles, including the peculiar logics underpinning detection, the relation between evidence and hypothesis, and the sometimes shifting roles and functions of the accused, witnesses, jury and judge, including the particular logic at the root of making, or extracting, a confession. Not all the exam questions are answered, though some are indirectly tackled within *Drama and Democracy*, for example those concerning Brecht and Koestler.

The imprint of New Crisis Quarterly revives the title of an exceedingly short-lived periodical: its first, only, and farewell issue appeared in 1984, under the guise of my *The Literary Labyrinth*. Its editorial programme was to publish reviews of books I didn't feel I had the time actually to write. Both the variously named reviewers and the variously authored reviewed books in *Literary Labyrinth* were therefore wholly imagined, but readers were invited, if so inclined, to write the books themselves.

Other NCQ books are rather more in the spirit of that editorial approach than this one, which is *almost* a proper book. But it too remains incomplete, not just in failing to answer all the exam questions, but because there are, of course, many other writers and issues not considered or even gestured at. So, in accordance with the original *NCQ* policy, readers are invited to undertake the rest of the exam themselves, especially, if I might suggest, those questions relating to Bienek, *The Cell*, Pinget, *The Investigation*, Williams, *The Volunteers*, and *Measure for Measure*. At the very least, you might undertake to update my examples, applications, precedents, or cases.

I want here to record long-standing debts to colleagues and friends, including several lawyers associated with the Kent Law Clinic, as well as Claire Palley, Brian Simpson, and Peter Fitzpatrick, and various historians and philosophers of science, including particularly Ernan McMullin, Olaf Pedersen, Mary Hesse, Alan Shapiro, and Michael Hoskin. Some of this material was apparently once used on the introductory courses for law students at the University of Lancaster. I deny all legal responsibility for any such use.

B.S.

STUDIES IN LEGAL FICTIONS

Finals Examination

A colleague had once declared that Philip ought to publish his examination papers. The suggestion had been intended as a sneer, but Philip had been rather taken with the idea --- seeing in it for a few dizzy hours, a heaven-sent solution to his professional barrenness. He visualized a critical work of totally revolutionary form, a concise, comprehensive survey of English literature consisting entirely of questions, elegantly printed with acres of white paper between them, questions that would be miracles of condensation, eloquence and thoughtfulness, questions to read and re-read, questions to brood over, as pregnant and enigmatic as haikus, as memorable as proverbs; questions that would, so to speak, contain within themselves the ghostly, subtly suggested embryos of their own answers. *Collected Literary Questions*, by Philip Sparrow. A book to be compared with Pascal's *Pensees* or Wittgenstein's *Philosophical Investigations*.

David Lodge

EXAM QUESTIONS

Course 007: Studies in Legal Fictions

Time allowed: THIRTY DAYS

There are FIFTEEN questions.
Candidates should answer QUESTION ONE and FIVE other questions, taken from any TWO other Sections. Not more than THREE questions may be taken from ANY ONE Section. Candidates are reminded that they are not permitted to duplicate either materials or methodological approaches in more than TWO questions but that they are encouraged to display throughout an overall epistemological consistency. Begin each answer in a fresh answer-book.

Section A: General Principles

1. 'The bases for our present legal procedures were first laid down in the mid-eighteenth century and were perfected by the late eighteenth century; from that short period stem almost all our current legal freedoms.' (J. P. HERBERT) Support, refute or modify this claim with reference to *either* Fielding, *Tom Jones, or* Godwin, *Caleb Williams*

Section B: Detection, Policing, and Prosecution

2. 'The private detective has no private privilege before the law; his means and methods of pursuit and prosecution must be, in principle, as public as those of the police proper.' (B. MALONE) Discuss the procedures of Poe's Dupin with particular reference to *The Mystery of Marie Roget.*

3. 'His Majesty's Secret Service must be above suspicion—and beyond reproach.' (H. M. CHARLES). How far does Sherlock Holmes go to meet these royal requirements in *A Scandal in Bohemia*?

4. 'Anarchy is not merely thoughtless—it is unthinkable.' (LORD CROMWELL). Would Father Brown agree? You may confine your discussion to *The Blue Cross.*

5. 'The naked truth is never visible to a voyeur.' (M. POWELL). Comment on the contribution of the cinema screen to our image of detection, with reference to *two of* the following: *Young Mr Lincoln, The Wrong Man, Peeping Tom.*

6. What confidence can be placed in the notion of a 'legitimation crisis'? Your answer should make some use of Raymond Chandler's *The Big Sleep.*

7. 'Everybody is always on trial.' (*attributed to:* S. KOBA). How far does this modem proverb illuminate *one* of the following *pairs* of novels:
(a) Alain Robbe-Grillet, *Les Gommes* and *L'Année derniere à Marienbad;*
(b) Robert Pinget, *L'inquisitoire* and *Le Fiston;*
(c) Stefan Themerson, *Special Branch* and *Wooff Wooff or Who Killed Richard Wagner?*

8. Is *The Volunteers,* by R. H. Williams, a 'private eye' novel?

Section C: Accusation, Perjury, and Confession

9. 'Only the accused knows, in the end, if he's guilty; that's the beauty of a British trial.' (J. SAMSA). Is Kafka's *Der Prozess* truly British?

10. In what ways might the Soviet legal system be seen as having pioneered a genuinely contem-porary concept of legality? You may *not* discuss Tertz, *The Trial Begins,* or Bienek, *The Cell,* or Koestler, *Darkness at Noon,* in your answer.

11. 'Normality is never on trial.' (G. THORP). How far is this un-true in Nossack, *The Impossible Proof?*

12. 'Let no man be judge in his own case unless he be as just as what I am.' (LORD JUSTICE DEVIAN). Does Camus's Clamence, in *The Fall,* judge himself, mercifully?

13. 'Accusation is the best form of defence.' (P. C. REGINALD-NIXON). In the light of this remark, comment critically on the plays of Peter Handke, especially *Offending the Audience* and *Self-Accusation.*

Section D: Trials and Responsibilities

4. 'Athens had no trained legal experts—only trained democrats. And slaves. And women.' (H. A. LENA). What relevance do the plays of Euripides have today?

15. List any *fifteen* plays by Brecht you consider appropriate.

Q. 1 : HENRY FIELDING, *Tom Jones*

> 'Jesu!' said the Squire, 'would you commit two persons to the bridewell for a twig? '
> 'Yes,' said the Lawyer, 'and with great lenity too; for if we had called it a young tree they would have been both hanged.'
>
> Fielding, *Joseph Andrews*

Let us begin with a once influential attempt at a theory of 'Law'. In his essay, 'Ideology and the Ideological State Apparatuses', Louis Althusser seeks to advance a clarification and modification of Marx's architectural metaphor of 'base and superstructure'. He first sketches that metaphor thus:

> Marx conceived the structure of every society as constituted by 'levels' or 'instances' articulated by a specific determination: the infrastructure, or economic base (the "unity' of the productive forces and the relations of production) and the superstructure, which itself contains two 'levels' or 'instances': the politico-legal (law and the State) and ideology (the different ideologies, religious, ethical, legal, political, etc.).[1]

In this formulation 'law' appears within the superstructure but not as 'ideology'. As Althusser outlines his own 'descriptive theory' of 'the State' the position of 'law' becomes progressively unclear. He offers a distinction between the Repressive State Apparatus and the Ideological State Apparatuses; the former, in one formulation, includes 'the Courts':

> Remember that in Marxist theory, the State Apparatus (SA) contains: the Government, the Administration, the Army, the Police, the Courts, the Prisons, etc., which

---

[1] L. Althusser, *Lenin and Philosophy*, New Left Books, 1971, p.129 (cited hereafter as *LP*)

> constitute what I shall in future call the Repressive State Apparatus. (*LP*, p.136)

On the same page, he states:

> we can for the moment regard the following institutions as Ideological State Apparatuses:
> —the religious ISA (the system of the different Churches),
> —the educational ISA (the system of the different public and private Schools),
> —the family ISA,
> —the legal ISA,
> —the political ISA (the political system, including the different Parties),
> —the trade-union ISA,
> —the communications ISA (press, radio and television, etc.),
> —the cultural ISA (Literature, the Arts, sports, etc.).
> I have said that the ISAs must not be confused with the (Repressive) State Apparatus.

But if 'the Courts' are listed with the RSA and 'the legal ISA' figures in the list of ISAs, is there not a certain 'confusion'? A footnote rather unhelpfully remarks:

> The 'Law' belongs both to the (Repressive) State Apparatus and to the systems of the ISAs.

Subsequent lists of the ISAs sometimes include the 'legal' (pp. 153, 156) and sometimes don't (though a casual 'etc.' can leave the list incomplete, as on p. 143).

The 'law' also seems, from one perspective, to stand 'outside' both RSA and ISAs and to make possible one distinction between them: Althusser justifies his use of 'State' in the term 'Ideological State Apparatuses', despite the apparently private nature of these institutions, on the grounds that 'the distinction between the public and the private is a distinction internal to bourgeois law, and valid in the (subordinate) domain in which bourgeois law exercises its "authority" ' (p. 137). He adds:

> the domain of the State escapes it [bourgeois law] because the latter is "above the law": the State, which is the State of the ruling class, is neither public nor private; on the contrary, it is the precondition for any distinction between public and private.

It's not clear how far Althusser himself is employing the notion of the State being 'above the law'; if the 'law' is itself a State Apparatus, how far is the State to be distinguished from the Apparatuses which constitute it?

Another distinction offered between RSA and ISAs is that the RSA 'functions massively and predominantly by repression (including physical repression), while functioning secondarily by ideology', while ISAs 'function massively and predominantly by ideology, but they also function secondarily by repression' (p. 138). It's then, of course, difficult to know just what is distinctive about 'repression' if it only 'includes' physical repression; nor is it clear how 'ideology' is to be distinguished from 'repression' if non-physical 'repression' isn't 'ideology'.

As we pursue the location of 'law' Althusser's distinctions become ever more confusing. He distinguishes 'ideology in general' from (regional) 'ideologies' (pp. 151, 156); but, according to his 'central thesis' (p. 159), 'the category of the subject (which may function under other names: e.g., as the soul in Plato, as God, etc.) is the constitutive category of all ideology', even if 'it only appears under this name [the subject] with the rise of bourgeois ideology, above all with the rise of legal ideology' —and another unhelpful footnote adds:

> Which [which??] borrowed the legal category of 'subject in law' to make an ideological notion: man is by nature a subject. (p.160).

A number of questions arise: for example, is 'legal ideology' (only) a 'region' of 'bourgeois ideology' (though the legal category of 'subject in law' would seem to predate even the 'rise' of 'bourgeois ideology')? And the crucial question—what does Althusser mean by 'subject'?—is never, to my mind, clarified in Althusser's text.

What particularly interests me here is the *slippery status* of 'law', 'the Law', 'legal ideology'—the different terms swim around in the text, and Althusser seems to have no clear idea of what he means by them or how, if at all, he differentiates between these terms, which perhaps isn't surprising since the legal process is never clarified or distinguished into its several practices, from legislation to sentencing.

In a later text, *Reply to John Lewis*, Althusser is equally slippery: 'this bourgeois ideology', he says, 'is actually in its *deepest essence* [my emphasis] constituted by the ideological pair economism/ humanism'.[2] This 'pair'

> is a pair in which the two terms are complementary. It is not an accidental link, but an organic and consubstantial one. It is born spontaneously, that is to say necessarily, of the bourgeois practices of production and exploitation, and at the same time of the legal practices of bourgeois law and its ideology, which provides a sanction for the capitalist relations of production and exploitation and their reproduction. (pp. 85-6)

'Ideas,' he goes on to say:

> find their foundations in the categories of Bourgeois Law and the legal ideology materially indispensable to the functioning of Bourgeois Law: liberty of the Person, that is, in principle, his right freely to dispose of himself, his right to his property. . . This is the breeding ground of economism/humanism: the capitalist mode of production and exploitation. And this is the precise link by which, the precise place in which these two ideologies join together as a pair: Bourgeois Law, which

[2] See L. Althusser, *Essays in Self-Criticism*, NLB 1976, p.85. (Cited hereafter as *ESC*)

at the same time both provides a real support for capitalist relations of production and lends its categories to liberal and humanist ideology, including bourgeois philosophy (*ESC* pp. 86-7).

It's difficult to know precisely what all this means. 'Bourgeois Law', it seems, provides the 'categories' of 'economism / humanism', and 'bourgeois ideology' borrows from 'legal ideology' the 'category' of 'subject in law', yet 'ideology [in general] has no history'—even though the 'category' of 'subject' is the 'constitutive category of all ideology' and that 'category' 'only appears under this name' with 'the rise of bourgeois ideology'.

Perhaps it is unfair to bring together in this way formulations from essays written three years apart, but the terminological counters that are being shunted around in the two essays seem to have at least a family resemblance to each other and one might therefore expect, if not compatibility between the essays, at least mutual illumination or specific clarification of differences. Yet all that remains, for this reader anyway, is a conceptual fog in what seems to be a crucial area for Althusser himself.

Some of that fog might be cleared slightly by taking two other formulations by Althusser and trying to 'test' them. Though 'ideology in general' 'has no history', Althusser nevertheless thinks that 'it is possible to hold that ideologies have a history of their own (although it is determined in the last instance by the class struggle)' (*LP*, p. 151). Presumably then, 'legal ideology'—if that is a 'regional ideology'—might have a history of its own.

Secondly, Althusser remarks that 'in the pre-capitalist historical period which I have examined extremely broadly, it is absolutely clear that there was one dominant Ideological State Apparatus, the Church' (*LP*, pp. 143-4), whereas now, he thinks, 'what the bourgeoisie has installed as its number-one, i.e. as its dominant ideological State apparatus, is the educational apparatus, which has in fact replaced in its functions the previously dominant ideological State apparatus, the Church' (*LP*, pp. 145-6). There might therefore be a 'history' of changes in the relative dominance of ISAs—though it is perhaps odd that Althusser should credit 'bourgeois law' and 'legal ideology' with such significance in providing crucial 'categories' yet not discuss their 'dominance' in any period.

Still, Althusser has a penchant for examining a historical period only 'extremely broadly', so perhaps a more detailed examination of a particular historical period can supplement, or even illuminate, his panoramic perspective.

ii

> In 1754 at Chelmsford the Chief Justice condemned a girl to hanging and dissection for murdering her baby. He had pressured the jury to bring in a simple verdict of guilty (at first they found her insane); but having exacted justice, he then expressed the helplessness of men before it: 'Before I pronounced the sentence,' he confided to his diary, 'I made a very proper speech *extempore* and pronounced it with dignity, in which I was so affected that the tears were gushing out several times against my will. It was discerned by all the company . . .and a lady gave me her handkerchief dipped in lavender water to help me.'

Douglas Hay, citing this incident,[3] comments:

> In its ritual, its judgements and its channelling of emotion the criminal law echoed many of the most powerful psychic components of religion. The judge might, as at Chelmsford, emulate the priest in his role of human agent, helpless but submissive before the demands of his deity. But the judge could play the role of deity as well, both the god of wrath and the merciful arbiter of men's fates. (*AFT*, p.29)

---

[3] In his essay 'Property, Authority and the Criminal Law' in *Albion's Fatal Tree*, ed. D. Hay, P. Linebaugh, & E. P. Thompson, Allen Lane 1975. (Cited hereafter as *AFT*)

Hay's essay examines the majestic ritual of the eighteenth-century English High Court circuit, the rhetorical power of the judge's Address to the Grand Jury and the righteous passion of his sentencing address to the condemned, the deliberate theatricality of the last-minute reprieve from the King, the paternalism and patronage of the gentry in supporting or ignoring petitions for mercy, and he places all these elements within a persuasive analysis of the crucial role of law, as legislative process and as repressive practice, in eighteenth-century England. At one point he analyses the relative strength accorded to religion and law in the ideological armoury of the ruling class, and concludes:

> Religion still had a place within the ritual of the law: a clergyman gave the assize sermon, and others attended the condemned man on the scaffold. But we suspect that the men of God derived more prestige from the occasion than they conferred on it. A suggestion of this can be seen in an evangelical pamphlet published in 1795. In the metaphors of power, judges usually had been likened to God, deriving their authority from divine authority, mediated through the Crown. But the author reversed the metaphor in his attempt to resurrect religion: he likened the deity to an English high court justice, and called the Day of Judgement the 'Grand Assizes, or General Gaol Delivery'. The secular mysteries of the courts had burned deep into the popular consciousness, and perhaps the labouring poor knew more of the terrors of the law than those of religion. When they did hear of hell, it was often from a judge. (*AFT*, p.30)

On the basis of Hay's analysis, we might suggest that—in Althusser's terms—in eighteenth-century England it was the legal apparatus which, for a time, replaced the religious apparatus as the 'dominant' 'ISA'. But we then have to be clearer as to what the term 'legal apparatus' denotes in the period.

In terms of court-practice, some pointers may help to ward off a reading-back of twentieth-century practice into the eighteenth. Charles Cottu, a French judge who toured the Northern Circuit, recorded a reaction, as late as 1822 which can help us to avoid anachronisms:

> The English appear to attach no importance to a discovery of causes which may have induced the prisoner to commit the crime: they scarcely even affix any to the establishment of his guilt. I am ignorant whether this temper of mind arises from their fear of augmenting the already excessive number of public offenders, or whether it proceeds from their natural humanity; it is however an undoubted fact, that they make no effort to obtain proofs of the crime, confiding its punishment entirely to the hatred or resentment of the injured party; careless too, about the conviction of the accused, whether his victim shall yield to feelings of compassion, or give way to indolence. (quoted by Hay, *AFT*, pp.40-1)

Most prosecutions for felony in the eighteenth century were 'private' prosecutions, brought by the injured party, who could decide for himself upon the severity of the charge; the accused was not allowed a defence counsel to plead to the jury; character-witnesses for the accused often carried much more weight than any material evidence concerning his guilt or innocence of the particular crime; judges had wide discretion in sentencing, extending even to complete pardon; an 'appeal' against sentence primarily took the form of petitions to the king, supported by personal letters from sympathetic gentry or aristocracy, often based quite explicitly on considerations of patronage or kinship-ties.

Hay interprets these various features of court-practice in terms of the complex patterns of local deference, loyalty and quasi-feudal dependency which still characterised the social and economic relations of rural and small-town life in eighteenth-century England. But, as he points out, these 'close and persisting personal relationships' did not obtain to the same degree in London, where, for example, 'judicial mercy . . was more often a bureaucratic lottery than a convincing expression of paternalism' (p. 55). One index to the difference between a rural parish and the metropolis was the prevalence in the capital of 'strawmen'—professional perjurers who could be regularly hired just outside the law-courts.

Hay's phrase 'bureaucratic lottery' hints however at a certain change which was becoming apparent in the legal-administrative procedures, and which was indeed to be advocated by the legal reformers: a regularisation and rationalisation of the relation between crime, charge and sentence.

The legal reformers Sir Samuel Romilly and William Eden both appealed, more or less explicitly, to the model proposed by Cesare Boccaria in 1764: 'a fixed code of laws, which must be observed to the letter' (see *AFT*, p. 57). But though English legal practice shied away from any such radical reform, it is arguable that a change of at least related significance did occur during the century. Towards the end of his detailed analysis of the origins and application of 'The Black Act' of 1723 (9 George I c. 22), E. P. Thompson remarks:[4]

> The Act registered the long decline in the effectiveness of old methods of class control and discipline and their replacement by one standard recourse of authority: the example of terror. In place of the whipping-post and the stocks, manorial and corporate controls and the physical harrying of vagabonds, economists advocated the discipline of low wages and starvation, and lawyers the sanction of death. Both indicated an increasing impersonality in the mediation of class relations, and a change, not so much in the 'facts' of crime as in the category—'crime'—itself, as it was defined by the propertied. What was now to be punished was not an offence between men (a breach of fealty or deference, a 'waste' of agrarian use-values, an offence to one's own corporate community and its ethos, a violation of trust

[4] E.P. Thompson, *Whigs and Hunters*, Allen Lane 1975, pp. 206-7 (cited hereafter as *WH*)

> and function) but an offence against property. Since property was a thing, it became possible to define offences as crimes against things, rather than as injuries to men. This enabled the law to assume, with its robes, the postures of impartiality: it was neutral as between every degree of man, and defended only the inviolability of the ownership of things

Thompson sees the early part of the century in terms of that 'recognised phase of commercial capitalism when predators fight for the spoils of power and have not yet agreed to submit to rational or bureaucratic rules and forms' (see *WH*, p. 197), when political and economic struggle within the ruling class is still shaped by networks of 'nepotism, interest and purchase' and fought out between followings of loyal dependents. The legal practices Hay analyses are in harmony with this phase.

But there is then a paradox in the practice of 'the law': if 'the law' were to 'assume, with its robes, the postures of impartiality' (and if it did not it would be less effective as an 'ideological' weapon against the ruled) and if at the same time it was effectively to redefine 'crimes' as offences against 'things' rather than as injuries to men, there would have to be an abandonment of those courtroom practices which so clearly treated prosecution, trial and sentencing as shaped primarily by the initiative, partiality and discretion of the 'injured party'. In their stead would emerge a reliance not upon testimony of 'character' but on evidence of specific actions, and a shift from private pursuit and prosecution to 'impersonal' and 'public' policing and prosecution. In certain respects the conditions of life in London had already suggested the need for such shifts: the trade of perjury made it inevitable that magistrates should pay more heed to material evidence, while the need for a publicly-financed police force where no local gentry held sway had long been apparent.

At the same time there was a more general paradox at the heart of eighteenth-century legal practice, which Thompson outlines in his concluding remarks:

> The work of the sixteenth- and seventeenth-century jurists, supported by the practical struggles of such men as Hampden and Lilburne, was passed down as a legacy to the eighteenth century, where it gave rise to a vision, in the minds of some men, of an ideal aspiration towards universal values of law. One thinks of Swift or of Goldsmith or, with more qualifications, of Sir William Blackstone or Sir Michael Foster. If we today have ideal notions of what law might be, we derive them in some part from that cultural moment. It is, in part, in terms of that age's own aspirations that we judge the Black Act and find it deficient. But at the same time this same century, governed as it was by the forms of law, provides a text-book illustration of the employment of law, as instrument and as ideology, in serving the interests of the ruling class. The oligarchs and the great gentry were content to be subject to the rule of law only because this law was serviceable and afforded to their hegemony the rhetoric of legitimacy. This paradox has been at the heart of this study. It was also at the heart of eighteenth-century society. But it was also a paradox which that society could not in the end transcend, for the paradox was held in equipoise upon an ulterior equilibrium of class forces. When the struggles of 1790-1832. signalled that this equilibrium had changed, the rulers of England were faced with alarming alternatives. (*WH*, p. 169)

Thompson himself, with the whole complexity of his study of the Black Act behind him, criticises 'a sophisticated but (ultimately) highly schematic Marxism' for which 'the law is . by definition a part of a "superstructure" adapting itself to the necessities of an infrastructure of productive forces and productive relations' (p.259). He proposes rather a complex and multi-faceted conclusion:

> The law when considered as institution (the courts, with their class theatre and class procedures) or as personnel (the judges, the lawyers, the Justices of the Peace) may very easily be assimilated to those of the ruling class. But

> all that is entailed in 'the law' is not subsumed in these institutions. The law may also be seen as ideology, or as particular rules and sanctions which stand in a definite and active relationship (often a field of conflict) to social norms; and, finally, it may be seen simply in terms of its own logic, rules and procedures—that is, simply as law. And it is not possible to conceive of any complex society without law. (*WH*, p. 260)

But though Thompson's target here is, fairly transparently, Althusser, there is at least a certain congruence between his phrase 'its own logic, rules and procedure—that is, simply as law' and Althusser's rather hesitant recognition that, possibly, 'ideologies have a history of their own'. Thompson indeed seems to echo some of Althusser's hesitations and difficulties when he remarks 'The greatest of all legal fictions is that the law itself evolves, from case to case, by its own impartial logic, true only to its own integrity, unswayed by expedient considerations' (*WH*, p. 250).

The problem is, clearly, that neither Althusser nor Thompson can conceive of a 'history' of 'law', even of its 'own logic, rules and procedures', that would not be intimately shaped by a wider 'history'; yet at the same time even Althusser hesitates before any ultimate 'reduction' of the 'legal' to total determination by the class struggle. But if Thompson is correct that 'it is not possible to conceive of any complex society without law', then even a socialist society will be faced with the problem of the law's 'logic, rules and procedures'. If he is also right that we have inherited from the struggles of the past 'an ideal aspiration towards universal values of law', an aspiration which we discard only at great political risk, it may be politically important to try to grasp the 'history' or 'logic' of 'law'—if we can isolate it to grasp.

Fully to 'isolate' legal ideology would be to produce a necessarily idealist account (perhaps a philosophy of law); it is in the practice of law that its problems of logic, rule and procedure always arise and are worked through—yet it is in the practice of law that it becomes inextricable from the wider history. How then are we appropriately to isolate 'law', 'simply as law'?

If we focus on one of the problems internal to legal practice which, it was suggested earlier, emerged in eighteenth-century England—the problem of evidence, of reconciling or combining reliance on 'personal' assessments of the accused's 'character' with an emphasis on 'impartial' and material evidence for the crime having been committed—we can perhaps recognise at least one instance of an attempt to probe the logic of that problem 'in isolation' from the concomitant pressures and considerations of actual legal practice: in the textual practices of Henry Fielding's novel, *Tom Jones*.

iii

Dorothy George once remarked that Fielding's 'appointment as a salaried Justice of the Peace for Westminster in 1749 was in its way as epoch-making as the appearance of *Tom Jones* in the same year.' That comment suggests a biographical point of intersection between text and legal apparatus which need only be indicated here in a fairly sketchy fashion.

Fielding first studied law at Leyden in his twenties (he was sent there in disgrace after an *affaire*), but his fairly successful period as a dramatist deflected him from any legal career for some time. Only after his satire on Walpole in his *The Historical Register for 1736* had prompted the retaliation of the Licensing Act of 1737 (under which all plays had to be licensed for performance by the Lord Chancellor), did Fielding return to the law, studying for the next few years at the Middle Temple. In 1740, at the age of thirty-three, he was called to the Bar and went on the Western Circuit.

The same year, however, the publication of Samuel Richardson's *Pamela* tempted him back to literature, first with the parody *Shamela* and then with a novel which grew more serious and ambitious as he wrote it, *Joseph Andrews*, published in 1742. The death of his wife very shortly after may have contributed to his decision in 1744 to abandon literature again—the decision was made public in his preface in July 1744 to Sarah Fielding's *David Simple.* He devoted himself instead to serious preparation for an ambitious scholarly treatise on Crown Law, which was, hopefully, to make his reputation.

The influence of these resumed legal studies can be seen in his next satire, celebrating the death of the old enemy Walpole, published in July 1745: *The Charge to the Jury: or. The Sum of the Evidence, on the Trial of A.B.C.D and E.F. All M.D. For the Death of one Robert at Orford.* This vein of political writing was continued in three anti-Jacobite pamphlets published the same year, and then from November 1745 to June 1746 he edited the pro-Government paper *The True Patriot.* Partly as a reward for this, and for his hand in *The Jacobite Journal*, Fielding was appointed Commissioner of the Peace for Middlesex in June 1747 and then Magistrate of the City and Borough of Westminster in July 1748.

Tom Jones, which was perhaps begun as early as January 1745, was published in early 1749. Later the same year Fielding published two pamphlets which considerably furthered his legal reputation, at least in some circles: *A Charge Delivered to the Grand Jury* and *A True State of the Case of Bosavem Penlez*. The following year his *Enquiry into the Causes of the Late Increase of Robbers*, published with a considerable sense of timing in January 1750, was warmly praised by some members of the House of Commons Committee on Law Reform, which sat from February 1750 to June 1751. It is from that Committee that Radzinowicz, in his great history of English law, dates the 'movement for reform' in English criminal law.

Tom Jones therefore can, and should, be placed within this immediate context: it was written during those very years when not only Fielding himself but the House of Commons and Fielding's Government patrons were deeply preoccupied with questions of law and legal reform (and, incidentally, with improving the provision of law-enforcement in London).

Fielding's predecessor as City Magistrate, Sir Thomas de Veil, had written his *Observations on the Practice of a Justice of the Peace intended for such Gentlemen as design to act for Middlesex or Westminster* as a result of reflecting upon his own term of office (a highly lucrative one in his case). It was published posthumously in 1747 and Fielding (who actually moved into Sir Thomas's old house) undoubtedly read it.

It may not be too much to claim that *Tom Jones*, if it was not actually a kind of substitute for the finally unwritten treatise on Crown Law, was at least in part the result of and partial equivalent to 'Observations' not dissimilar to Sir Thomas's. It is time we looked at the text itself.

iv

Early in *Tom Jones*,[5] there is a characteristic paragraph:

> As this is one of those deep observations which very few readers can be supposed capable of making themselves, I have thought proper to lend them my assistance; but this is a favour rarely to be expected in the course of my work. Indeed I shall seldom or never so indulge him, unless in such instances as this, where nothing but the inspiration with which we writers are gifted can possibly enable any one to make the discovery. (I, v. p. 38)

Since the 'observation' commented upon is hardly a 'deep' one, the playful irony is clear; but its reverberations are not, as yet. On the following page we read:

> The sagacious reader will not from this simile imagine that these poor people had any apprehension of the design with which Mrs Wilkins was now coming towards them; but as the great beauty of the simile may possibly sleep these hundred years till some future commentator shall take this work in hand, I think proper to lend the reader a little assistance in this place. (I, vi. p.39)

[5] References are given to Book & Chapter, with page refs. to the 1963 Signet edition.

The shift from 'sagacious reader' to plain 'reader' puts the actual reader in a dilemma of self-definition: if 'sagacious' he should not need the commentary in the next paragraph; as 'reader' he, of course, reads it. And when the simile is finally given in ultimately prosaic form, 'to say the truth, she was universally hated and dreaded by them all', that touch of authorial assistance only alerts us to be sceptical of its 'truth' since we have already been warned, however ironically, that only 'deep observations' will merit such assistance.

Both the question of 'truth' and the distinction between kinds of reader are constantly being brought to our attention as we read. Book II, Ch. i, for example, speaks of not being afraid to leave 'a chasm in our history', where 'no matters of consequence occurred' (p.65). Book III, Ch. i, retrospectively notes that such gaps give the reader 'an opportunity of employing that wonderful sagacity of which he is master by filling up these vacant spaces of time with his own conjectures; for which purpose we have taken care to qualify him in the preceding pages' (p.97), and Fielding outlines how 'the judicious reader' will have filled in two of those gaps, 'as examples only of the task which may be imposed on readers of the lowest class', but, he warns, 'much higher and harder exercises of judgement and penetration may reasonably be expected from the upper graduates in criticism' (p.98).

Some of these 'harder exercises' clearly concern the 'truth' of what Fielding, as narrator, tells the reader. He attributes two motives to Jenny but adds, teasingly, 'But though this latter view, if indeed she had it, may appear reasonable enough . . . ' (I, ix. p.48). He offers his own temptingly 'judicious' judgement: 'whether the captain acted by this maxim, I will not positively determine; so far, we may confidently say that his actions may be fairly derived from his diabolical principle...' (I, xiii. p. 61). He alerts the unalert reader to apparent problems and suggests apparent solutions: 'I have thought it somewhat strange, upon reflection, that the housekeeper never acquainted Mrs Blifil with this news . . The only way, as it appears to me, of solving this difficulty . . ' (II, v. p.77).

He even declares his own 'bias' in a way that reinforces the tactic of special pleading: 'Though I called him poor Partridge in the last paragraph, I would have the reader rather impute that epithet to the compassion of my temper than conceive it to be any declaration of his innocence' (II, vi. p. 84). And, clearly, our judgement throughout is being invited, exercised, and manipulated concerning what is being narrated, the major incidents of the novel.

But the hardest 'exercise' of all, perhaps, is most deeply buried in the text. In Book XII, Ch. viii. Fielding comments:

> For instance, as the fact at present before us now stands without any comment of mine upon it, though it may at first sight offend some readers, yet upon more mature consideration it must please all; for wise and good men may consider what happened to Jones at Upton as a just punishment for his wickedness with regard to women . . and silly and bad persons may comfort themselves in their vices by flattering their own hearts that the characters of men are rather owing to accident than to virtue. Now, perhaps the reflections which we should be here inclined to draw would alike contradict both these conclusions, and would show that these incidents contribute only to confirm the great, useful, and uncommon doctrine which it is the purpose of this whole work to inculcate and which we must not fill up our pages by frequently repeating, as an ordinary parson fills his sermon by repeating his text at the end of every paragraph. (p. 554)

That 'great, useful, and uncommon doctrine' is, of course, never explicitly formulated, let alone frequently repeated.

But the essential clue is immediately given, for those readers who still require a clue, at the beginning (of course!) of the next paragraph:

> We are contented that it must appear, however unhappily Sophia had erred in her opinion of Jones, she had sufficient reason for her opinion . . .

Fielding has taken care to provide Sophia with 'sufficient reason' for her erroneous opinion, just as he has provided the reader with 'sufficient reason' for both agreeing and disagreeing with Fielding's 'own' judgements, interpretations and 'erroneous opinions'; but by this stage in reading the novel, we also realise that 'sufficient reason' is never 'sufficient' for proof, for 'truth' rather than 'opinion': we can never be sure that we know enough, or know the right evidence, for a final judgement—and yet we are forced to judge, always on insufficient 'sufficient reason'. We are forced to judge, to make up our own minds both in attributing motives and in reconstructing events, because the relationship with the narrator, established by the devices of style instanced above, puts us in that position—but the 'position' is not a single or simple one.

At times it's as if we were judge or jury, weighing evidence and witnesses we have to recognise may be untrustworthy; at other moments, we find ourselves placed in the position of defence counsel, making a plea of mitigation or objecting to and protesting at a particularly tendentious interpretation of the 'evidence' by the prosecuting counsel (a role correspondingly assumed, at that same moment, by Fielding or one of his character-witnesses); and all the time we ought to know ourselves to be on trial, our own capacity for judgement is in the dock: are we a 'judicious reader' (III, i. p.98), an 'over-zealous' reader (III, iv. p. 106) or just a plain, and inadequate, 'reader'? The only 'truth' we can be sure of is that Fielding puts that mildly accusing question to us; but we can't even be sure of the answer.

Tom Jones, then, can be read as creating a relation which shiftingly situates both 'author' and 'reader' in roles and practices whose closest analogue is the roles and practices of the legal apparatus, analysed not directly in terms of its repressive and ideological functions but (to use Thompson's formulation) 'simply in terms of its *own logic, rules and procedures*'. But at the same time, precisely in putting those roles and practices in a kind of constant disarray, the text discloses and produces possibilities not available in actual legal practice: we (both author and reader) have the option of switching and straddling legal roles and of subverting or endorsing legal practices within the operation of the novel.

These possibilities are open because, crucially, the relation is fictional and so are the case, evidence and witnesses we judge: our necessary judgements have no consequences except upon ourselves (the 'closure' of the novel ensures that our judgements do not affect what is 'already written', which itself in any case ensures a suitably 'happy ending').

This absence of responsibility then allows a further possibility: that the *basic premise* of the law's 'own logic, rules and procedures' can be put in question. Precisely because the novel offers a fictional exercising of judgement (relaxation) and not an exercise in real judgement (responsibility) it can *admit* that legal judgement is based on insufficient 'sufficient reason' since 'the truth' can never be known to be known. But the law rests finally on the assumption that the truth can be made public, even if it is the 'private' truth of motive ('I swear to tell the truth ...').

At this point, of course, the text, like the legal apparatus itself, is traversed by elements derived from a different ideological apparatus, the religious. If, as Thompson puts it, the law became in the eighteenth century 'the central legitimizing ideology, displacing the religious authority and sanctions of previous centuries' (*WH*, p.263), the logic of court rules and procedures still sought validation, foundation and legitimisation in religious ideology ('I swear . . so help me God') since if perjury has no meaning neither do witnesses.

Tom Jones recuperates certainty at the level of arbitrary or predestined 'given' character (Tom is ultimately good, Blifil irredeemably bad) and thereby links hands with a code derived from another tradition, the Literary Romance, and with one crucial element in the ideology of the Religious Apparatus.

Fielding articulates both basic strategies in his 'own' comments on his relation to his readers:

> Reader, I think proper, before we proceed any further together, to acquaint thee that I intend to digress

> through this whole history as often as I see occasion; of which I am myself a better judge than any pitiful critic whatever. And here I must desire all those critics to mind their own business, and not to intermeddle with affairs or works which no ways concern them; for till they produce the authority by which they are constituted judges, I shall not plead to their jurisdiction. (I, ii. p.31).

> For all which I shall not look upon myself as accountable to any court of critical jurisdiction whatever; for as I am, in reality, the founder of a new province of writing, so I am at liberty to make what laws I please therein. And these laws my readers, whom I consider as my subjects, are bound to believe in and obey [but] I do not, like a *jure divino* tyrant, imagine that they are my slaves or my commodity. I am, indeed, set over them for their own good only, and was created for their use and not they for mine. (II, ii, p.66)

The limits are marked, but breakable: the reader is both subject of a benevolent creator who can ordain the constitution of his world as he sees fit, and is also (dangerously) a potential critic of the basic law of that world, the truth and authority of its creator.

Yet the process of reading the text is, deliberately, a training in the undermining of the authority of that maker ('for which purpose we have taken care to qualify him in the preceding pages', p.97). In the curious 'social relation' which constitutes the text it is acceptance of authority which is given, but scepticism of authority which is produced.

In creating that fictional relation Henry Fielding, Esq., the concrete individual, can clearly be seen as 're-working' the professional situation of Mr. Justice Fielding, barrister and magistrate, towards an impossible resolution, a re-arrangement of role, practice and responsibility possible only for 'Henry Fielding', the writer of this novel.

To achieve that, he must in the process 'create' another, a reader who endorses and collaborates in that re-arrangement, that disarray of the apparatus, but who may, for that very reason, become even more subversive than its author. Whereas Mr. Justice Fielding was clearly caught in certain acute contradictions in his own professional practice and opinions—visible in the tension between his strict application of the law as it stood, while acting on the bench, and his emergent awareness in his professional writings of a 'social' perspective on the causes of crime—the reader of *Tom Jones* is curiously privileged: while the reading process obtains, that transformation of the practices of the legal apparatus remains available to him, perhaps even as a promise of an eventual actual transformation.

V

This sketch of an analysis of *Tom Jones* is, of course, only a partial account. The complex interaction of religious and legal ideological elements in the text would have to be investigated further, and it would be necessary to place the whole novel within a much broader context of other literary texts—not least those other eighteenth-century literary works which reveal a preoccupation with facets of 'the law', ranging from *The Newgate Calendar* through *The Beggars' Opera* to Fielding's own *Jonathan Wild the Great.*

One writer who might be interestingly compared with Fielding, on both counts, is Daniel Defoe, since a case can be made that at least some of Defoe's novels are constructed as reworkings of certain codes and practices of the Religious Apparatus (the relation of *Moll Flanders* to a tradition of 'case-law' in the theological-moral system of casuistry is an obvious example).

What needs overall emphasis in this context is how closely the combination of 'religious' and 'legal' elements in *Tom Jones* reproduces the intersection of different practices and procedures in the London law-courts of the mid-eighteenth century. Like the reader of *Tom Jones*, the London magistrate, particularly, had to judge each character who came before him both in terms of their 'innate' moral character—perhaps visible to the trained and judicious eye even in their surface appearance, but, if not, able to be revealed by some superior person in a convenient note—

and on the basis of whatever 'hard evidence' could be discovered.

The one practice relied, in the end, on rank prejudice; the other claimed the authority of rational procedures. But neither, in the long run, provided the lower classes with truly sufficient reason for trusting in the omniscience and impartiality of 'the Law'. They had learned their lesson, in practice, only too well for that.

*

Q. 2: EDGAR ALLAN POE, *The Mystery Of Marie Roget*

> The story is told of an automaton constructed in such a way that it could play a winning game of chess, answering each move of an opponent with a countermove. A puppet in Turkish attire and with a large hookah in its mouth sat before a chessboard placed on a large table. A system of mirrors created the illusion that this table was transparent from all sides. Actually, a little hunch-back who was an expert chess player sat inside and guided the puppet's hand by means of strings. One can imagine a philosophical counterpart to this device. The puppet called 'historical materialism' is to win all the time. It can easily be a match for anyone if it enlists the services of theology, which today, as we know, is wizened and has to keep out of sight.
>
> Walter Benjamin, *Theses on the Philosophy of History*

In April 1841 *Graham's Magazine* published a short story by Edgar Allan Poe entitled *The Murders in the Rue Morgue*. At a stroke, so the familiar account goes, Poe had invented the detective story, and his central character, C. Auguste Dupin, immediately established the prototype for a long list of fictional sleuths.

The second of the Dupin trilogy was published in the *Snowden Ladies' Companion* for November and December 1842 and February 1843. It was entitled *The Mystery of Marie Roget: a sequel to The Murder in the Rue Morgue*. Of this second tale, Poe himself wrote, in a letter to Dr J. E. Snodgrass in June 1842:

> The story is based upon that of the real murder of Mary Cecilia Rogers, which created so vast an excitement some months ago in New York. I have handled the design in a very singular and entirely novel manner. A young grisette, one Marie Roget, has been murdered under precisely similar circumstances with Mary Rogers. Thus under pretence of showing how Dupin (the hero of the Rue Morgue) unravelled the mystery of Marie's assassination, I, in fact, enter into a very rigorous

> examination of the real tragedy in New York. No point is omitted. I examine, each by each, the opinions and arguments of our press on the subject, and show (I think satisfactorily) that this subject has never yet been approached. The press has been entirely on a wrong scent. In fact, I really believe, not only that I have demonstrated the falsity of the idea that the girl was the victim of a gang, but have indicated the assassin. My main object, however . . is the analysis of the principles of investigation in cases of like character. Dupin reasons the matter throughout.

It is the notion that Dupin 'reasons the matter throughout' that can claim our attention first.

Six years earlier, Poe had already demonstrated what he regarded as the workings of 'reason'—the application of observation and logic to the solution of a 'mystery'—in his explanation of the 'mechanism' of a chess-playing 'Automation', in *Maelzel's Chess-Player* (*The Southern Literary Messenger*, April 1836). At one point in that essay Poe singles out an attempt at explanation by an anonymous writer who 'by a course of reasoning exceedingly unphilosophical, has contrived to blunder upon a plausible solution —although we cannot consider it altogether the true one.'

Basically, the anonymous writer had tried to show that the partitions of the box, at which the automation chess-player sat, could be so manipulated as to conceal from view a hidden human chess-player, even during the 'demonstration' by Maelzel that the box did not contain any human agency. 'There can be no doubt', writes Poe:

> that the principle, or rather the result of this solution is the true one. Some person is concealed in the box during the whole time of exhibiting the interior. We object, however, to the whole verbose description of the manner in which the partitions are shifted to accommodate the movements of the person concealed. We object to it as a mere theory assumed in the first place, and to which circumstances are afterwards made to adapt themselves. It was not, and could not have

> been, arrived at by any inductive reasoning. To show that certain movements might possibly be effected in a certain way, is very far from showing that they are actually so effected. There may be an infinity of other methods by which the same result may be obtained . . The probability of the one assumed proving the correct one is then as unity to infinity.

Poe counterposes to the anonymous writer's argument a two-fold strategy. First, he argues that the 'mechanism' of the Automaton must indeed be a human rather than a mechanical agency since the very nature of a chess game rules out a mechanical player:

> Arithmetical or algebraical calculations are, from their very nature, fixed and determinate. Certain data being given, certain results necessarily and inevitably follow. These results have dependence upon nothing but the data originally given. And the question to be solved proceeds, or should proceed, to its final determination, by a succession of unerring steps liable to no change, and subject to no modification. This being the case, we can without difficulty conceive the possibility of so arranging a piece of mechanism that upon starting it in accordance with the data of the question to be solved, it should continue its movements regularly, progressively and undeviatingly towards the required solution, since these movements, however complex, are never imagined to be otherwise than finite and determinate. But the case is widely different with the Chess-Player. With him there is no determinate progression. No one move in chess necessarily follows upon any one other. From no particular disposition of the men at one period of a game can we predicate their disposition at a different period . . from the first move in the game of chess no especial second move follows of necessity. In the algebraical question, as it proceeds towards solution, the certainty of its operations remains altogether unimpaired. The second step having been a consequence of the data, the third step is equally a

> consequence of the second, the fourth of the third, the fifth of the fourth, and so on, and not possibly otherwise, to the end. But in proportion to the progress made in a game of chess, is the uncertainty of each ensuing move. A few moves having been made, no step is certain. Different spectators of the game would advise different moves. All is then dependent upon the variable judgment of the players. Now even granting (what should not be granted) that the movements of the Automaton Chess-Player were in themselves determinate, they would be necessarily interrupted and disarranged by the indeterminate will of his antagonist. There is then no analogy whatever between the operations of the Chess-Player and those of the calculating machine.

Second, to establish how the human agency is brought to bear, Poe offers a series of 'observations' of the routine which Maelzel 'invariably' follows in exhibiting the interior of the box. Poe's explanation is deemed to be convincing because

> if it were observed that never, in any single instance, did M. Maelzel differ from the routine we have pointed out as necessary to our solution, it would be one of the strongest possible arguments in corroboration of it—but the argument becomes infinitely strengthened it we duly consider the circumstance that he does occasionally deviate from the routine, but never does so deviate as to falsify the solution.

Poe's own solution need not detain us at all, but from this article on Maelzel's Chess-Player we can single out three strands: that a more or less correct solution may not be supported by correct reasoning; that a human agency is required by, and is implicated in, a pattern of unpredictable moves; and that only accurate observation can provide the data for a correct theory to build upon.

In *The Mystery of Marie Roget* it is clear that Poe is attempting to apply a similar process of ratiocination to the solution of a crime; but the story in practice violates at least two of the principles *Maelzel's Chess-Player* relied upon.

If a correct solution can be 'supported' by incorrect reasoning, a demolition of that incorrect reasoning does not thereby establish that the conclusion is incorrect: that Socrates is mortal remains true even if the argument offered in support of it is invalid (e.g. 'The gods are immortal; Socrates is not a god; therefore Socrates is mortal'). Yet Dupin spends quite some time in Marie Roget demonstrating that the argument of the newspaper *L'Etoile* is fallacious; *L'Etoile* had sought to show that the body recovered from the river could not be Marie's; Dupin shows that their argument is incorrect, but this can in no way, of itself, show that the body recovered is Marie's. To 'establish' that, Dupin has to appeal to an identification by a witness—and at that point introduces another principle (the calculus of probabilities) to which we can return.

Within the text the ostensible reason for even entering upon the argument as to whether the body is really Marie's or not, is that G—, the Prefect, has made a 'liberal proposition' to Dupin for his help in solving the mystery, but Dupin distrusts G— sufficiently to realise that the (presumably pecuniary) proposition might not be honoured if the precise terms of the assignment are not met: to find the assassin of Marie Roget. A a living Marie Roget or the assassin of someone else would not bring the reward. In the text, the reward offered to the public amounts to 30,000 francs, and the fact of this large reward is later to play a part in establishing that the murder was not committed by a gang.

At this point, we have to take account of Poe's claim that *Marie Roget* is based on the case of Mary Cecilia Rogers and that no point of relevance is omitted. Presumably, therefore, an equally large reward had also been offered in the case of Mary Rogers. In his letter to Snodgrass Poe claims to have indicated the assassin; he would therefore, according to his own reasoning, be in at least a very strong position to claim the offered reward—and this makes his offering of his solution to the Mary Rogers case as a public fiction rather peculiar. If Poe were really convinced by his own arguments, what was to stop him from publishing them as conclusive contributions to the real case? Fears of committing libel may have played a part, or even a reluctance to work outside the 'due process' of police arrest and formal trial; but there are other reasons, both why the parallels are not pressed to the point of actually identifying the murderer and why *Marie Roget* is, necessarily, offered as fiction.

The ostensible reasons are clear in the text. The text in fact breaks off at the point where 'the murderer will be traced' and an editorial note (ostensibly by the editors of *Snowden Ladies Companion*) is inserted:

> For reasons which we shall not specify, but which to many readers will appear obvious, we have taken the liberty of here omitting, from the MSS placed in our hands, such portion as details the following up of the apparently slight clew obtained by Dupin. We feel it advisable only to state, in brief, that the result desired was brought to pass; and that the Prefect fulfilled punctually, although with reluctance, the terms of his compact with the Chevalier. Mr. Poe's article concludes with the following words.—Eds.

Poe, in concluding the story, comes close to covering himself against any possible libel action by, first, a disclaimer and then by an appeal (again) to the Calculus of Probabilities: he notes the parallel with Mary Rogers, but adds:

> But let it not for a moment be supposed that, in proceeding with the sad narrative of Marie from the epoch just mentioned, and in tracing to its *dénouement* the mystery which enshrouded her, it is my covert design to hint at an extension of the parallel, or even to suggest that the measures adopted in Paris for the discovery of the assassin of a grisette, or measures founded in any similar ratiocination, would produce any similar result.
>
> For, in respect to the latter branch of the supposition, it should be considered that the most trifling variation in the facts of the two cases might give rise to the most

> important miscalculations, by diverting thoroughly the two courses of events; very much as, in arithmetic, an error which, in its own individuality, may be inappreciable, produces, at length, by dint of multiplication at all points of the process, a result enormously at variance with truth. And, in regard to the former branch, we must not fail to hold in view that the very Calculus of Probabilities to which I have referred, forbids all idea of the extension of the parallel—forbids it with a positiveness strong and decided just in proportion as this parallel has already been long-drawn and exact.

But the notion that there might be even a 'most trifling variation in the facts of the two cases' brings us back to Poe's letter to Snodgrass. On the basis of the claims made there, one could say that Poe was satisfied that no 'trifling variation' could overthrow his analysis. But on what is that analysis based?

In a note added to the tale on its reprinting some years later, Poe states that it 'was composed at a distance from the scene of the atrocity, and with no other means of investigation than the newspapers afforded'. The strategy of the tale is to reproduce this dependence on newspaper reports: after Dupin has agreed to look into the case the narrating 'I' is sent to procure at the Prefecture 'a full report of all the evidence elicited, and, at the various newspaper offices, a copy of every paper in which, from first to last, had been published any decisive information in regard to this sad affair'. Though occasional appeals are made thereafter to the authority of the police file, the reader is not allowed 'direct access' to any documentary information apart from that contained in the newspaper reports, which are quoted at length.

Clearly, the implication of this device is that the reader is on an equal footing with Dupin in trying to solve the mystery. But is that footing a secure one for either? At one point Dupin notes, of *Le Commerciel*, that its 'deductions from the premisses are philosophical and acute; but the premisses, in two instances, at least, are founded in imperfect observation.' But then even if Dupin's (and Poe's) own 'deductions from the premisses are philosophical and acute' the trustworthiness of his conclusions will depend on the 'observations' which support them—but he relies upon newspaper reports for his 'observations', his data.

And, as Dupin himself remarks, 'we should bear in mind that, in general, it is the object of our newspapers rather to create a sensation—to make a point—than to further the cause of truth. The latter end is only pursued when it seems coincident with the former.' More specifically, he notes that the papers have been silent on a number of questions of importance: 'had the body been in any respect despoiled? Had the deceased any articles of jewellery about her person upon leaving home? If so, had she any when found?'

Clearly, the newspapers are not necessarily reliable as sources of 'observation' in the first place. We can see in this, perhaps, one reason why Poe, himself dependent upon newspaper reports, could not risk being publicly conclusive about the real case but resorted to a fictionalised version. But if the newspapers are not necessarily reliable, doesn't that raise a question about the strategy of offering long extracts to the reader?

The problem here is that the ostensible strategy of the tale is the classic device of the 'detective story': that the reader is given all the necessary clues and is therefore in a position to test his or her own deductive powers against those of the detective. The implication that in the real case the newspapers may not have picked up all the clues is clear from the tale itself: not only that, but at least one reader of those newspapers is shown not to have noticed all the clues they do contain: the narrating 'I' claims to have acquired a copy of 'every paper in which . . any decisive information' has been published, but when Dupin himself scours those same papers he selects five items which seem 'irrelevant' to the narrator (it was therefore a matter of chance that he procured those newspapers in the first place). Only in the light of Dupin's 'explanation' do these five 'extra' items come to appear relevant.

But, of course, the reader is not taken into the process of selection. The singling out and presentation of precisely these items is *already* governed by the explanation which they are offered to us as supporting. In other words, the actual process which guides Dupin to fix upon these items as relevant is not given; all we are offered is the finished conclusion which shapes these items into a connected pattern. The peculiar problem here is that *if* these items are indeed relevant, then the explanation offered is 'reasonable', but *only* if the explanation is *already* regarded as reasonable can the items be singled out as more relevant than any others.

This interdependence of 'data' and 'theory' has some parallel with one aspect of the argument offered in *Maelzel's Chess-Player*, that a machine can only operate within 'algebraic' moves, whereas no move in chess dictates the next move. Given that the newspapers for the three weeks or so between the murder and Dupin's investigation had published numerous other items and had not published accounts of all the incidents that had occurred on or about the time of the murder, any process of 'reasoning' based upon the reports that happened to appear in the press could only be like trying to play chess against an opponent not all of whose pieces or moves are known to one.

In other words, the 'reasoning' that Dupin is depicted as relying upon involves a large element of what we can call, for the moment, 'hunch' or 'intuition', while the 'observation' on which it is based is necessarily shaped to a large extent by what we can call, for the moment, 'chance' or 'accident'.

The reader, however, is not in the same position as Dupin. The reader is not, of course, given access to any 'extra' item in the newspapers which Dupin has already dismissed as irrelevant; the selection is already made for us, according to criteria of relevancy which are 'retrospective'—i.e. only when the explanation has already 'emerged' for Dupin does he offer these extra items for our consideration. Yet this practice is necessarily in contradiction with the principles which Dupin himself articulates to justify looking for those extra items in the first place:

> Not the least usual error in investigations such as this is the limiting of inquiry to the immediate, with total disregard of the collateral or circumstantial events. It is the malpractice of the courts to confine evidence and discussion to the bounds of apparent relevancy. Yet experience has shown, and a true philosophy will always show, that a vast, perhaps the larger, portion of truth arises from the seemingly irrelevant.

But how then is Dupin different from a court? By singling out these items he too confines 'evidence' and 'discussion' to what appears relevant to him.

Clearly, a *reductio ad absurdum* could be pursued here: at each point at which the 'bounds' of relevancy are drawn, one could claim that the 'truth' will be discovered only by going outside those bounds to the 'collateral or circumstantial'. In terms of the tale, when Dupin says to the narrator 'I will examine the newspapers more generally than you have as yet done', it is open to the reader to wish to examine those same newspapers (the real ones in the real case of Mary Rogers) 'more generally' than Poe has done.

But even without this move, Dupin's principle runs into a certain contradiction. He extends his argument to cover the operations of 'science':

> It is through the spirit of this principle, if not precisely through its letter, that modem science has resolved to calculate upon the unforseen. But perhaps you do not comprehend me. The history of human knowledge has so uninterruptedly shown that to collateral, or incidental, or accidental events we are indebted for the most numerous and most valuable discoveries, that it has at length become necessary, in any prospective view for improvement, to make not only large, but the largest, allowances for inventions that shall arise by chance, and quite out of the range of ordinary expectation. It is no longer philosophical to base upon what has been a vision of what is to be. Accident is admitted as a portion of the substructure.

But part of his own argument relies upon the exclusion of 'accident'. He argues that Marie must have intended to elope because she asked her fiancé to call for her at her aunt's after dark, thus allowing her till that time to arrange her elopement. That an accidental encounter with her former lover (or with anyone else) could have made her change her mind about going to her aunt's is simply not considered. The possibility of a chance meeting with her murderer has indeed to be ruled out for Dupin's whole thesis (linking the naval officer, Madame Deluc, and the boat) to hang together. (Of course, on his own principle that the more 'ordinary' a case, the more difficult it becomes to solve: a murder which arose from an entirely accidental encounter between two strangers would be insoluble—at least by ratiocination.)

Dupin completes the elaboration of his 'principle' with the comment that 'We make chance a matter of absolute calculation. We subject the unlooked for and unimagined to the mathematical formulae of the schools.' This formulation echoes three other points in the tale. The whole tale opens with the statement:

> There are few persons, even among the calmest thinkers, who have not occasionally been startled into a vague yet thrilling half-credence in the supernatural, by coincidences of so seemingly marvellous a character that, as mere coincidences, the intellect has been unable to receive them. Such sentiments—for the half-credences of which I speak have never the full force of thought —such sentiments are seldom thoroughly stifled unless by reference to the doctrine of chance, or, as it is technically termed, the Calculus of Probabilities. Now this Calculus is, in its essence, purely mathematical; and thus we have the anomaly of the most rigidly exact in science applied to the shadow and spirituality of the most intangible in speculation.

The final paragraph of the tale returns to this 'Calculus' to justify the assertion that a single 'trifling variation in the facts of the two cases' would rule out a transference of the solution to one to the other. The passage quoted above concerning the 'long-drawn and exact' parallel continues:

> This is one of those anomalous propositions which, seemingly appealing to thought altogether apart from the mathematical, is yet one which only the mathematician can fully entertain. Nothing, for example, is more difficult than to convince the merely general reader that the fact of sixes having been thrown twice in succession by a player at dice, is sufficient cause for betting the largest odds that sixes will not be thrown in the third attempt. A suggestion to this effect is usually rejected by the intellect at once. It does not appear that the two throws which have been completed, and which now lie absolutely in the Past, can have influence upon the throw which exists only in the Future.

This double appeal to the Calculus of Probabilities provides the tale with a framework of scientific and mathematical 'reasoning', insinuating that the reasoning exemplified within the tale is also 'scientific'.

At one point Dupin does indeed appeal to scientific knowledge, in order to demolish *L'Etoile*'s assumption that a corpse will not float to the surface until six to ten days after being thrown into the sea, but this demolition—as we have seen—in no way contributes positively to the solution of the case. The calculus of probabilities is also appealed to within the tale in order to demonstrate that the accumulation of identifying features of the corpse constitutes 'proof not added to proof, but multiplied by hundreds or thousands'—but Dupin is in any case prepared to accept M. Beauvais's identification of Marie without any supporting evidence:

> Nothing is more vague than impressions of individual identity. Each man recognises his neighbour, yet there are few instances in which anyone is prepared to give a reason for his recognition. The Editor of *L'Etoile* had no right to be offended at M. Beauvais's unreasoning belief.

But if ‘unreasoning belief’ is legitimate in the case of identification, how far is it also legitimate elsewhere? Dupin himself rules out suspicion of Beauvais: ‘In respect to the insinuations levelled at Beauvais, you will be willing to dismiss them in a breath. You have already fathomed the true character of this good gentleman. He is a busybody.’ But what if the reader regards this ‘fathoming’ of ‘character’ as an ‘unreasoning belief’ and as therefore illegitimate?

My point is, of course, that if the ‘reasoning’ whereby Dupin arrives at his solution were truly a matter of ‘scientific’ calculation in the sense implied by the appeal to mathematics and calculus, there would be no need to have recourse to such agreed ‘fathoming’ at any point. Yet, equally, insofar as Dupin's reasoning is based on a selection of data which derives (as far as the reader is concerned) *from* that reasoning, it is irrelevant whether the reader ‘agrees with’ the reasoning or not: the evidence offered the reader has already been shaped by that reasoning and would not be made available were it incompatible with the solution proposed.

The reader, in other words, is not on an equal footing with Dupin, though the whole strategy of the tale is to make it appear that he or she is. On the contrary, as readers we have to accept the authority of Dupin, both about the ‘character’ of suspects and about the ‘relevance’ of evidence. The tale itself indicates the model on which its own strategy is ultimately based:

> That Nature and its God are two, no man who thinks will deny. That the latter, creating the former, can, at will, control or modify it, is also unquestionable. I say ‘at will’; for the question is of will, and not, as the insanity of logic has assumed, of power. It is not that the Deity cannot modify his laws, but that we insult him in imagining a possible necessity for modification. In their origin these laws were fashioned to embrace all the contingencies which could lie in the Future. With God all is Now.

The law, the logic, of Dupin's 'reasoning' is God-like, at least in principle. His mode of reasoning will indeed embrace 'all contingencies' because it can, at will, 'control or modify' them; it has no need to, since the tale is, already, 'created' by its teller in accordance with that reasoning; nothing can lie 'in the Future', not even the throw of a dice, that has not already been 'fashioned' to fit that will, that 'reasoning'.

What distracts the reader from this recognition that the tale and its God are 'two', the latter wholly controlling the former, is precisely the claim that this tale is modelled, point for point, upon the real. As we register the added footnotes which identify the characters and newspapers of the tale with their real-life counterparts in the Mary Rogers case we extend that identification to the whole tale, including the reasoning of Dupin: because that reasoning 'works' within the tale, it would 'work' also in the real world of actual crime and corpses. One important facet of the realist aesthetic of much nineteenth-century fiction is embedded here: that the 'fathoming' of 'character' and the (moral) 'reasoning' that works in the fiction also works in real life. But, more to my purposes at this point, some of the possible permutations of the operations of 'detecting crime' are also embedded in the tale.

It is clear that *only* in a fiction can the 'reasoning' fully shape the 'data' 'in advance'. Poe's recommendation that a writer should write 'backwards' is apposite here:

> Nothing is more clear than that every plot, worth the name, must be elaborated to its *dénouement* before anything be attempted with the pen. It is only with the *dénouement* constantly in view that we can give a plot its indispensable air of consequence, or causation, by making the incidents, and especially the tone at all points, tend to the development of the intention.
>
> Poe, *The Philosophy of Composition*, 1846

It is also clear, in the tale, that the process of detection is not, whatever Dupin's or Poe's claims, a process of pure deduction from the data. At some point a 'hunch' intervenes, binding data and hypothesis together. It's also clear that if the observations on which the 'deduction' is founded are unreliable, the conclusion will be questionable.

Within the 'bounds' of a fiction (everything within those bounds being 'relevant'), some 'observations' can be 'reliable', the reader can be offered 'data' which, within the conventions of the tale itself, is to be taken as trustworthy (that Poe's data is 'literally translated' from actual newspapers opens up the space for the reader to question his data in this tale). But where, in a real case of detection, is such 'reliable observation' to be located? Poe, Dupin and the reader are all in the same position of being 'at a distance from the scene of the atrocity, and with no other means of investigation than the newspapers offered', but those intervening sources of observation are themselves shown to be unreliable within the tale.

Think now of the position of a jury in an actual criminal case. They too are, necessarily, 'at a distance' from the scene of the crime; they too have to rely upon intermediary 'observations'; they too have to reconstruct the crime and decide upon the criminal on the basis of data offered to them, by the accused, by witnesses, by counsel, and — crucially in most cases—by the police.

The police, now, are responsible for 'detection', for 'solving' a crime, for arresting the criminal; by that very fact, they are responsible for formulating the initial case against the accused, and the accused would not be in the dock (in theory) unless there were a reasonable hypothesis that he is the criminal.

Yet at the same time the 'presumption' that formally operates in most legal systems is that the accused is innocent until 'found' guilty, the onus of 'proof' being upon the prosecution. But if the 'proof' in question cannot be a rigorously 'scientific' proof, but rather a 'hypothesis' that 'embraces all contingencies', that most closely 'fits' the 'evidence', then endemic in the process of detection-prosecution is a tendency towards fiction, towards a situation where the 'reasonable' hypothesis can 'control or modify' the 'data' 'at will', a process of selection and arrangement which operates retrospectively, a plotting backwards. Endemic in the logic of detection-prosecution is therefore a fictional urge: to 'plant evidence', to 'frame', to 'manufacture' a case, to 'fit' the already-selected 'criminal' to the crime, and vice-versa.

Within a detective fiction, while the convention holds that the 'observations' the reader is initially offered are indeed reliable, the reader and the detective-figure are, in principle, on an equal footing; the process of 'plotting backward' will be rendered visible to the alert reader, the 'data' allowing the 'hypothesis' to emerge increasingly into the open. It's perhaps worth suggesting that if that convention of reliability begins to crumble, the 'hypothesis' that controls the 'data' of the tale will become less visible, less open and accessible, more entirely a matter of the author's operating 'at will'. This permutation might be explored in a number of later texts (for example, those of Robert Pinget).

It may also be worth suggesting that, similarly, if a convention that the police are 'reliable' begins to be eroded, the same kind of process may occur: the tendency towards 'fictional' control will be reinforced—either the 'hypothesis' will become increasingly comprehensive, extending to more and more 'collateral' circumstances, or the 'data' will become increasingly 'modified' to fit the hypothesis, and both these processes may become more covert, more concealed from even the alert inquirer.

If, also, at the core of the data-hypothesis bond in detection is, necessarily, a 'hunch' or 'intuition', and if acceptance of a particular bonding of data and hypothesis depends upon a belief in the competence or authority of the 'detective', then an erosion of confidence in that competence or authority may reinforce a tendency to conceal the process of arriving at that hunch.

There is a double paradox here: that an erosion of belief in authority may lead to a greater degree of imposed reliance on that authority, and that a suspicion of the unreliability of evidence may result in the provision of even less reliable evidence.

Some facets of this 'logic', of these paradoxes or contradictions within the process of detection-prosecution, have perhaps been seen (or rather not seen) at work recently, for example in political 'deportation' cases (the inclusion of collateral circumstances, the extension of 'relevancy'), in trials concerned with the Official Secrets Act (the gap between any detailed evidence and the overall charge being filled merely by the authoritative assertion of a 'danger to security'), and in the operation of the emergency legislation in Northern Ireland (the word of a senior police officer taken as sufficient 'evidence' for internment). In some post-modernist detective fiction a related logic is clearly at work: as the relation between event and pattern becomes more and more a matter of authorial discretion, only an increased assent to authorial authority can entice the reader to trust in the eventual emergence of any pattern at all.

In relation specifically to Poe's tale, however, there are some further points worth brief consideration. The conclusion of Dupin's process of reasoning is not given in the tale; the 'editorial note' intervenes instead. But the added prefatory footnote states:

> It may not be improper to record . . that the confessions of two persons (one of them the Madame Deluc of the narrative), made, at different periods, long subsequent to the publication, confirmed, in full, not only the general conclusion, but absolutely all the chief hypothetical details by which that conclusion was attained.

For the reader concerned with the verisimilitude of the tale, these subsequent confessions, operating from 'outside' the text, serve to confirm in advance (the footnote precedes the tale) the precise mapping of fiction onto reality, endorsing and ratifying the ratiocination of Dupin.

However, for the reader concerned with the *logic* of the tale, the confessions can only be an 'accident': they lie outside not only the text itself but also the chain of reasoning of the text; a 'deduction' and a 'confession' may be in parallel, but the logic of a third-person account is not the logic of a first-person account—though certain strategies of detective-fiction may seek to fuse them: deduction by 'psychology', or, more radically, by the detective proving in the end to be the criminal. At the very least, the starting-points of a first- and third-person account are formally different, even though in the construction of the fiction ('plotting backward') they are the same: the logical starting-point is always a knowledge of the criminal.

But what secure 'confirmation' could there be, other than a confession? Given the problems of linking data and hypothesis, an 'intuition' is necessarily unreliable—only knowledge can bridge that epistemological gap, and only the criminal has that 'knowledge'; but unless we are ourselves the criminals, we have that knowledge only by proxy.

We may, of course, arrive at the correct solution, even by incorrect reasoning; conversely, even correct reasoning may give us a wrong solution; only a form of knowledge that requires the mediation of neither observation nor reasoning could be self-validating. But, of course, even a confession may be 'false'. Most of us, however, would believe even a false confession—unless we had learned to suspect even the reliability of 'confessions' too.

Joseph Wood Krutch remarked of Poe that he 'invented the detective story in order that he might not go mad'. It seems a bizarre comment, even if a certain amount of biographical data might support such an hypothesis. But considering the problems of 'scientific' reasoning that have been touched upon so far, the suggestion is worth considering.

The text certainly reveals an awareness of the paradox of the 'Calculus of Probabilities': 'thus we have the anomaly of the most rigidly exact in science applied to the shadow and spirituality of the most intangible in speculation'. But it is not by mathematics or the calculus that Dupin arrives at his conclusions, but rather by a process that I have so far talked of in terms of data-hypothesis bonding, that bonding being achieved by a 'hunch' or 'intuition'. The last two terms seem unsatisfactory, but what others are we to use?

The difficulty arises partly because the very process those terms point to is hidden from us, in the tale itself. Dupin reads all the newspapers 'more generally', we are told; he emerges from that reading with five items not noticed up to then by the narrator. Why those five items? They operate as crucial links in Dupin's chain of explanation, but how did he recognise them as such in the first place? The text does not, and arguably cannot, tell us. The actual construction of the hypothesis and its simultaneous (?) selection-and-connecting of the 'relevant' data (relevant now to itself, to the hypothesis) is a moment which is absent from the text. In one sense that 'moment' must lie 'outside' the text, since in this case we are not even given the final formulation of the hypothesis itself: that is covered over by the editorial intervention. The reader could, of course, ask himself or herself in what sense that fusion of data and (an) hypothesis has occurred at all—for him or herself as a reader, trying to both match and anticipate Dupin's conclusions.

Yet as far as the text is concerned there is only a jump in the chain of reasoning—signalled, perhaps, in a kind of displacement, by that *non-sequitur*: 'We have attained the idea either of a fatal accident under the roof of Madame Deluc'—the 'fatal accident' being introduced for the first time in this 'summing up'. If we allow the terms 'hunch' and 'intuition' to designate that absence 'in' the text, they may be acceptable enough. But if we introduce two other texts by Poe, as 'collateral' circumstances, we may see that there is a deeper problem.

In *Maelzel's Chess-Player* Poe argued that the chess-player must be manipulated by a human being since a machine could only handle strictly 'fixed and determinate' calculations, whereas in chess 'a few moves having been made, no step is certain', so that 'different spectators of the game would advise different moves' and 'all is then dependent upon the variable judgment of the players'. But why is the judgement of the players 'variable' and in what sense? And why couldn't a machine play chess? Clearly, whatever the answers to these questions, for Poe, the human brain does not necessarily proceed by 'fixed and determinate' calculations.

In another text Poe tried to explore one process of the human brain, his own—in writing a poem. Poe's account of his writing of *The Raven*, in *The Philosophy of Composition* (1846), is designed 'to render it manifest that no one point in its composition is referrible either to accident or intuition—that the work proceeded, step by step, to its completion with the precision and rigid consequence of a mathematical problem'.

The essay reads, however, much more like an account of someone playing chess, facing a sequence of choice-points at each of which, out of a possible set of options, the player chooses one; but at least in the account as given, the specific choices made by Poe are not arrived at by a comparative consideration of the merits of all the other possible choices. One example of this (absence of) procedure can suffice:

> The sound of the refrain being thus determined, it became necessary to select a word embodying this sound, and at the same time in the fullest possible keeping with that melancholy which I had predetermined as the tone of the poem. In such a search it would have been absolutely impossible to overlook the word 'Nevermore'. In fact, it was the very first which presented itself.

That phrase 'presented itself' indicates the problem. If this was not 'accident' or 'intuition', it certainly wasn't arrived at 'step by step . . with the precision and rigid consequence of a mathematical problem'. It was 'arrived at', perhaps, the way 'steps' are themselves arrived at in a mathematical problem, or the way a word is 'arrived at' when we speak, or, maybe, the way a word 'presents itself' when 'we' make a slip of the tongue, pen or typewriter. And we have no full account of how any of those processes happen, despite the best efforts of Chomsky and Freud.

However, it is the ambition, the 'design', which governs this essay that most intrigues me: the urge to give a 'scientific' account of the process of 'composition'. (It is not irrelevant that the essay could be considered the precursor of a long line of inquiries into the construction of poetry, that Poe's own *poetique* has its recent progeny, and that his Dupin story *The Purloined Letter* had a certain status among Lacanian Freudians). Let me put alongside this ambition another, perhaps thinly-veiled, ambition:

> There are ideal series of events which run parallel with the real ones. They rarely coincide. Men and circumstances generally modify the ideal train of events, so that it seems imperfect, and its consequences are equally imperfect.

The implication of that passage is that if 'men and circumstances' would somehow cease interfering, the 'ideal series of events' would have a free run in the world. It's a peculiarly idealist notion of history, among other things. It's also the view of some who seem to believe that they know what the 'ideal series of events' is, in other words, what the 'real' ought to be. In one sense, a commitment to an 'ideal train of events' seems inescapable, unless one is simply to be a fatalist. But there is perhaps a worrying overtone in this particular formulation, with its suggestion that a world without 'men and circumstances' would be a more 'ideal', a less 'imperfect' world.

Such an ideal world is envisaged in a famous parable by Lichtenberg. It is the dream of a certain kind of scientist, whose admiration for the laws of physics and for mathematical order is tempered only by the realisation that 'men and circumstances' are, regrettably, not similarly 'fixed and determinate', or at least that to render them so would require the grasp of a law and order we do not yet have fully at our disposal.

These rather impressionistic reactions to that brief quotation are undoubtedly unfair to Novalis, from whom the passage is taken; but the passage was first selected by Poe—as the epigraph to *The Mystery of Marie Roget* and in that context some of the responses that 'presented themselves' above seem not entirely inappropriate. For Dupin, at least, seems to prefer, on the whole, to live in an 'ideal' world, without the intrusions of men and circumstances:

> Upon the winding up of the tragedy involved in the deaths of Madame L'Espanaye and her daughter, the Chevalier dismissed the affair at once from his attention, and relapsed into his old habits of moody reverie.

> Prone, at all times, to abstraction, I readily fell in with his humour; and continuing to occupy our chambers in the Faubourg Saint Germain, we gave the Future to the winds, and slumbered tranquilly in the Present, weaving the dull world around us into dreams. . . Strange as it may appear, the third week from the discovery of the body had passed . . before even a rumour of the events which had so agitated the public mind reached the ears of Dupin and myself. Engaged in researches which had absorbed our whole attention, it had been nearly a month since either of us had gone abroad, or received a visitor, or more than glanced at the leading political articles in one of the daily papers.

It would be interesting to know precisely what Dupin's 'politics' were. But it would be even more interesting to know just what Poe (or 'I') meant by that curious phrase quoted earlier: 'the insanity of logic'—or perhaps that was just a slip of the quill.

However, rather than take the option now of exploring those (related) problems, I want, finally, to return to a phrase from *Maelzel's Chess-Player*. There, Poe had castigated the anonymous writer's method of explanation as 'a mere theory assumed in the first place, and to which circumstances are afterwards made to adapt themselves'. Poe should have attended to his own criticism.

For there is a further 'gap' or 'absence' in the case of *The Mystery of Marie Roget*—its absence from the January 1843 issue of the *Snowden Ladies' Companion* (see above). According to John Walsh, in his *Poe the Detective*, it was only after the publication of the first two parts that Poe became aware that the accumulation of evidence in the case of Mary Cecilia Rogers pointed not to a murder by a former lover, a naval officer, but rather to a bungled abortion. Publication of the third part of the tale was held back for a month while Poe tried to salvage his detective's 'reasoning'. But attempts to adapt the new 'circumstances' to the theory he had assumed in the first two parts could only result in that symptomatic *non-sequitur*, that sudden intrusion of a fatal accident, and in a specious 'editorial' intervention. Even six years later, however, Poe could still refer, with apparent authority, to the 'naval officer' whom his theory had once selected as the necessary criminal (letter to George W. Eveleth, 4th January, 1849).

In a brief note, *On Intuition*, Poe once remarked: 'Great intellects guess well. The laws of Kepler were, professedly, guesses.' That aside, 'professedly', marks his hesitation and reluctance in actually acknowledging that at the centre of the 'mystery' of 'reasoning' may be what we can still only call 'guessing'—and even a Dupin doesn't always guess well. Such an admission could only be a scandal to a mind so firmly wedded as Poe's was, professedly, to a mid-nineteenth century belief in 'the most rigidly exact in science'. It might even have led him to wonder whether his whole 'philosophy' was not, in a rather painfully literal sense, abortive.

*

Q.3: SIR ARTHUR CONAN DOYLE, *A Scandal in Bohemia*

—There's no police like Holmes.
James Joyce.

Fifty years after the first Dupin story was published, the first Sherlock Holmes short story, *A Scandal in Bohemia*, appeared in *The Strand Magazine* for July 1891 (the two earlier Holmes novels, *A Study in Scarlet* and *The Sign of Four*, had not been particularly successful). Holmes's character rather obviously echoes that of Dupin: Holmes 'loathed every form of society with his whole Bohemian soul', so spends his time 'buried among his old books, . . alternating from week to week between cocaine and ambition, the drowsiness of the drug, and the fierce energy of his own keen nature'; only when he is 'hot upon the scent of some new problem' does Holmes rise 'out of his drug-created dreams'.

Dupin's method, of detection is also clearly echoed, but with a certain twist to it. Watson, the first-person narrator, tells us: 'He was, I take it, the most perfect reasoning and observing machine that the world has seen', but 'observation' is now supplemented by a deliberate collecting of 'data': Holmes 'for many years . . had adopted a system of docketing all paragraphs concerning men and things, so that it was difficult to name a subject or a person on which he could not at once furnish information'.

Even if one leaves aside the problem of accommodating such a universal data-bank within the confines of a modest Baker Street flat, one might at least query that curious phrase: 'all paragraphs concerning men and things'. All paragraphs from what sources? A second-hand omniscience seems peculiarly vulnerable to the vagaries of rather less 'perfect' observing machines than Mr. Holmes. One might also raise an eyebrow at the librarianship that could devise an index to such a collection. Surely only a fictional file could live up to these specifications, and the only appropriately qualified custodian for the filing-cards would be the Recording Angel himself.

Holmes's 'reasoning' is equally problematic. Watson, taken aback by his friend's remark, 'In practice again, I observe', asks 'How do you know?' Holmes's bland reply 'I see it, I deduce it' covers, by a mere comma, the process of fusing observation and deduction. The demonstration of Holmes's powers that follows is revealing: '. . . if a gentleman walks into my rooms smelling of idioform, with a black mark of nitrate of silver upon his right forefinger, and a bulge on the side of his top hat to show where he has secreted his stethoscope, I must be dull indeed if I do not pronounce him to be an active member of the medical profession.'

The gullible reader may for a moment be tempted to remark, with Watson, 'When I hear you give your reasons . . the thing always appears to me to be so ridiculously simple that I could easily do it myself, though at each successive instance of your reasoning I am baffled, until you explain your process.' But, of course, the reader could not 'do it', since the information which supports the conclusion is only given at the same time as, or even after, the conclusion. For the reader, there is nothing to see in the first place, though the precise visual details incorporated in the 'reasons' sometimes have the curious effect of persuading readers that they really have failed to 'notice' the obvious. Watson functions here not so much as a surrogate for the reader but rather as a decoy for the memory of the reader: we are enticed into attributing to ourselves an obtuseness we were never in a position to be guilty of.

Watson can sometimes, of course, function simply as a direct stand-in for the reader: Holmes 'threw over a sheet of thick pink-tinted note-paper which had been lying open upon the table. 'It came by the last post,' said he. 'Read it aloud'. . ' It is not for Holmes's benefit that that 'aloud' is included in the order; as Holmes himself remarks, he — or rather the plodding technician Conan Doyle — 'would be lost without my Boswell'. The device of inserting the dull-witted pawn Watson between Holmes and the reader is crucial to the manipulative strategy of Doyle. Like Poe, he cannot give the reader access either to all the relevant 'observations' or, fully, to the detective's process of 'reasoning' — until the two can be triumphantly presented as already fused into a 'solution'.

But it is not this rather primitive and now-tired device that is initially of interest in this story, since the progress of this tale rests not upon any 'deductive reasoning' at all but upon a simple trick. Holmes baldly states his aim: 'I will get her to show me', and this is to be achieved by engineering access to Irene Adler's house and arranging a false fire alarm. All that is necessary to achieve this is money, a fair amount of it to pay for the various actors in the little drama Holmes stages, plus a casual, gentlemanly disregard for the law: 'You don't mind breaking the law?' asks Holmes; 'Not in the least', replies the good Dr. Watson.

Already in the initial exchange with the King of Bohemia concerning the recovery of the 'scandalous' photograph, Holmes had suggested money and law-breaking as equally acceptable methods:

> 'It must be recovered.'
> 'We have tried and failed.'
> 'Your Majesty must pay. It must be bought.'
> 'She will not sell.'
> 'Stolen, then.'
> 'Five attempts have been made. Twice burglars in my pay ransacked her house. Once we diverted her luggage when she travelled. Twice she has been waylaid. There has been no result.'
> Holmes laughed. 'It is quite a pretty little problem', said he.

The 'pretty little problem' is, to put it naively, how to prevent Irene Adler telling the truth about the King of Bohemia. The king is about to be royally married and 'a shadow of a doubt as to my conduct would bring the matter to an end.' Naturally, such conduct as burglary and assault is unobjectionable when the perpetrator is the King of Bohemia, and that he has 'cruelly wronged' a mere actress need cast no doubt on his conduct. Holmes shows no qualms about accepting the commission to aid this royal hypocrisy, though the good Dr. Watson does have a momentary moral tremor — soon stilled, however, by a familiar excuse:

> I do not know whether he [Holmes] was seized with compunction at that moment for the part he was playing, but I know that I never felt more heartily ashamed of myself in my life than when I saw the beautiful creature against whom I was conspiring, or the grace and kindliness with which she waited upon the injured man. And yet it would be the blackest treachery to Holmes to draw back now from the part which he had entrusted to me. I hardened my heart and. took the smoke rocket from under my ulster. After all, I thought, we are not injuring her. We are but preventing her from injuring another.

And Holmes himself, once foiled by Ms. Adler, allows himself a certain scepticism with regard to the monarch's unselfconscious self-esteem: 'Is it not a pity she was not on my level?' 'From what I have seen of the lady, she seems, indeed, to be on a very different level to Your Majesty,' said Holmes coldly— adding nevertheless 'I am sorry that I have not been able to bring your Majesty's business to a more successful conclusion.' And even though Holmes declines to take the king's hand in a farewell shake ('turning away without observing the hand which the King had stretched out to him' — even Holmes's observational powers can be suspended), there is no indication that he declined to take, and keep, the 'three hundred in gold, and seven hundred in notes' he had been paid.

The rather grubby morality of this tale, including its overt sexism, would not be worth attention, were it not that the intermittent ambivalencies of attitude within the tale indicate a certain unease about its own premisses, and we can perhaps trace in them a pretty enough pattern.

At the overt level, the tale endorses a number of obvious double-standards: for example, the king can break the law which others are to abide by; the male can 'wrong' a woman but her attempt to declare that wrong puts her in the wrong. But there is another, slightly less explicit, double-standard embedded in the tale. At one point Watson, conscientiously aping the methods of his mentor, scrutinises the 'sheet of thick pink-tinted notepaper' and discerns 'a large *E* with a small *g*, a *P*, and a large *G* with a small *t* woven into the texture of the paper.' 'What do you make of that?' asked Holmes. 'The name of the maker, no doubt; or his monogram, rather.' 'Not at all. The *G* with the small *t* stands for Gesellschaft,' which is the German for 'Company'.'

It's that immediately dismissive 'Not at all' which makes explicit a distinction which is fundamental to the operation of the text: a statement by the authoritative Holmes necessarily has more value than any statement by the stumbling Watson, even when Watson's guess is patently correct. Watson is right: 'EgPGt' is indeed the abbreviated name of the 'maker'; Holmes, with access to his reference books, can be somewhat more precise, but he is not thereby justified in so dismissing Watson's answer; it is, after all, the basis of his own. Watson, however, is rarely allowed to get even this close to rivalry with his master; his normal position is as mere foil, largely superfluous except as mediator for the reader (there is even no need for Watson to take part in the little melodrama outside Adler's house — any paid hack could have thrown the smoke rocket).

Right from the beginning of the tale a distinction between Holmes and Watson is erected which firmly locates them in their differential positions within a hierarchy:

> [Holmes] never spoke of the softer passions, save with a gibe and a sneer. They were admirable things for the observer — excellent for drawing the veil from men's motives and actions. But for the trained reasoner to admit such intrusions into his own delicate and finely adjusted temperament was to introduce a distracting factor which might throw doubt on all his mental results. Grit in a sensitive instrument, or a crack in one of his own high-power lenses, would not be more disturbing than a strong emotion in a nature such as his. . . I had seen little of Holmes lately. My marriage had drifted us away from each other. My own complete happiness, and the home-centred interests which rise up around the man who first finds himself master of his

> own. establishment, were sufficient to absorb all my attention.

Watson, clearly, is deeply contaminated by the 'softer passions'; a doubt is correspondingly thrown upon all his 'mental results'.

The reader, too, is fixed within this hierarchy (whatever his or her actual susceptibility to passions, soft or otherwise), since it is a premise of the tale that Holmes will always be more correct, more 'perfect' at reasoning and observing, than the reader. If necessary, such differential success can always be ensured by withholding evidence or mere manipulation of the plot. And that hierarchy is further extended, by the tale, to include the police:

> He was still, as ever, deeply attracted by the study of crime, and occupied his immense faculties and extraordinary powers of observation in following out those clues, and clearing up those mysteries, which had been abandoned as hopeless by the official police.

(The broad parallels to *The Purloined Letter* further tend to imply this contrast between Holmes and. the less-than-competent police, as for example in the echoes of the remark: 'They did not know how to look.') Holmes is not only superior to the police; he is absolved from the legal constraints that govern their official work. He, like the King of Bohemia, regards himself as privileged, as able to create his own private laws. It may be no accident that Holmes is first introduced to us as having a 'Bohemian soul'.

There is a final element in this play of double-standards and hierarchy: in most detective fiction the overriding priority of the text is to arrive at the truth, to disclose the guilty, to explain what, despite misleading or opaque appearances, really happened. *Scandal in Bohemia*, on the contrary, concerns an attempt to keep the truth hidden, and there is no mystery at all about what happened. Insofar as the 'truth', in the form of the concealed photograph, is to be uncovered, it is only in order that the larger truth, the story of the affair, should be even more securely 'hidden' from view, and whereas in most detective stories the task is to 'solve' a crime already committed, this tale concerns the committing of a crime to prevent a possible 'crime' from being committed. *Scandal in Bohemia* overturns and reverses conventional priorities.

One can phrase these points rather differently. If it is important that justice should not only not be done but that it should not even be seen not to be done, the best way may be to employ an 'agent' (the text's own term for Mr. Holmes) who can and will operate outside the 'official' law and 'if necessary' in contravention of that official law. It may also help if that agent swears to 'absolute secrecy' and operates in disguise. Of course, the rationale for creating such a hierarchy of law-enforcement agencies (even if some of them break the law) is often the 'need' to 'prevent a crime'.

It would obviously be a help, in preventing all possible crime, if a data-bank were kept of all possible criminals — though insofar as any-one just might one day become a 'criminal', the ideal data-bank would have at least a 'paragraph' on everyone. If such an ideal were, unfortunately, impractical, at least a comprehensive index of all those persons who clearly fit into suspect categories would be a feasible compromise.

> 'Kindly look her up in my index, Doctor', murmured Holmes. . . 'Let me see,' said Holmes. 'Hum! Born in New Jersey in the year 1858. Contralto — hum! La Scala, hum! Prima donna Imperial Opera of Warsaw — Yes! Retired from operatic stage — ha! Living in London — quite so!'

From such observations an immediate deduction follows, naturally. Of course, an agency which built up such a filing system might have a few other uses — not least that of preventing any unpleasant truths emerging which might cast a 'shadow of doubt' on the conduct of those who authorise, condone and finance theft and violence in their own interests.

Were, *per impossibile*, such an agency ever to operate outside the fictional world of scandals in Bohemia, the ordinary citizen might find him- or herself in an ambivalent position. Faced, perhaps, with a claim that some matter 'is of such weight that it may have an influence upon European history', it might seem churlish to refuse the role of dumb pawn; would it not be 'the greatest treachery' (perhaps to 'the most perfect . . machine that the world has seen') to refrain from — metaphorically speaking, of course — hurling the rocket? After all, perhaps 'we are but preventing her from injuring another'.

The Watsons of this world are, after all, definitely rather lesser beings, compared with the highly trained and ruthless professionals:

> From time to time I heard some vague account of his doings: of his summons to Odessa in the case of the Trepoff murder, of his clearing up of the singular tragedy of the Atkinson brothers at Trincomalee, and finally of the mission which he had accomplished so delicately and successfully for the reigning family of Holland. Beyond these signs of his activity, however, which I merely shared with all the readers of the daily press, I knew little . .

On the other hand, perhaps the more one knows about the other side of the case ('The King may do what he will without hindrance from one whom he has cruelly wronged. I keep it only to safeguard myself, and to preserve a weapon which will always secure me from any steps which he might take in the future.'), the more one might, just possibly, be tempted into recognising a certain degree of truth, even beauty, in the designated criminal (and victim). Even the agent himself might conceivably be tempted, perhaps at an unconscious level:

> . . it was close upon four before the door opened, and a drunken-looking groom*[sic]*, ill-kempt and side-whiskered with an inflamed face and disreputable clothes, walked into the room . . . .

> . . my lucky appearance saved the bride-groom from having to sally out into the streets in search of a best man . . .

— though all he may end up with may be mere cash from both sides, or perhaps a faded image of the truth, both fetishes:

> 'The bride gave me a sovereign, and I mean to wear it on my watch-chain in memory of the occasion.'

And:

> 'I am immensely indebted to you. Pray tell me in what way I can reward you. This ring —' He slipped an emerald snake ring from his finger and held it out upon the palm of his hand.
> 'Your Majesty has something which I should value even more highly,' said Holmes.
> 'You have but to name it.'
> 'This photograph.'
> The King stared at him in amazement.
> 'Irene's photograph,' he cried. 'Certainly, if you wish it.'

Perhaps even those who loath every form of society can be attracted by the ever-elusive image of a real *Eirene* (the well-educated Holmes's unconscious presumably spoke Greek), but it is surely a sad thought that even those who are instruments in his Majesty's warlike secret service might have to run the risk of such seduction.

We Watsons are, however, happily privileged, are we not? If, once in a while, our home-centred interests happen to prove insufficient to absorb all our attention, we can observe, with suitably ambivalent fascination, and even amusement, but without any real involvement, the (mainly fictional) activities (at least the more overt ones) of those who are dedicatedly seeking a final solution. After all, we live in an open and a secure society, where the police observe the laws and the criminals are clearly distinct from them — and no mere pawn in a staged drama is going to invade the privacy of our home, still less throw a rocket through our windows.

And if they do, it'll be a false alarm — won't it?

*

> The next period in the development of the police, from 1870 to 1920, saw three major changes. There was the extension of police activity into working class areas; internal reforms like record-keeping, improvements in conditions of work and pay; and the start of detection after the event, with the formation of the Criminal Investigation Department . . at Scotland Yard. . .From the 1870s records were kept of all reported crime . .
>
> A study of the feasibility of centralising police records in a national computer system was started in 1964 . . The computers ordered, three Burroughs 6700s, have the capacity to hold up to forty million records — one for every member of the adult population. Each of the 800 police stations in England and Wales is linked to the computer [at Police National Computer Unit (PHUC), Hendon] by a Visual Display Unit (VDU), a teleprinter, and, in emergency, there is the standby facility to dial into the computer via the local exchange. . . The criminal names index will include not only those convicted of a criminal offence but also those suspected of having committed an offence — the designation 'first came to notice' will be used. . . .
>
> It is estimated that by 1979 the computer will hold on file some 36,525,000 names / entries. These will include amongst others: Vehicles 26,000,000; Fingerprints 3,250,000; Suspended sentences 110,000; Criminal names 6,700,000.. . In 1965 it was estimated that the Special Branch held records on more than two million people in this country. The number is now nearer three million though most of these warrant only an index card ...
>
> Tony Bunyan, *The Political Police in Britain,* 1976

Q. 4: G. K. CHESTERTON, *The Blue Cross*

> A Dadaist is utterly unimpressed by any serious enterprise and smells a rat whenever people stop smiling and assume that attitude and those facial expressions which indicate that something important is about to be said.
>
> Paul Feyerabend, *Against Method*

> The Dadaists attached much less importance to the sales-value of their work than to its uselessness for contemplative immersion. The studied degradation of their material was not the least of their means to achieve this uselessness. What they intended and achieved was a relentless destruction of the aura of their creations, which they branded as reproductions with the very means of production.
>
> Walter Benjamin, *The Work of Art in the Age of Mechanical Reproduction*

> ... in accordance with then current Oxford practice, he [H. L. A. Hart] frequently likens laws to rules of games, as if laws constituted social life's contests in the way that rules constitute games; a sporting view of things, certainly.
>
> Anthony Skillen, *Ruling Illusions*

Half-way through *A Scandal in Bohemia* (1891) Sherlock Holmes

> disappeared into his bedroom, and returned in a few minutes in the character of an amiable and simple-minded Nonconformist clergyman. His broad black hat, his baggy trousers, his white tie, his sympathetic smile, and general look of peering and benevolent curiosity, were such as Mr. John Hare alone could have equalled.

Twenty years later, the great Valentin, head of the Paris police and the most famous investigator in the world, encountered on an English train 'a very short Roman Catholic priest going up from a small Essex village'—and almost laughed:

> The little priest was so much the essence of those Eastern flats: he had a face as round and dull as a Norfolk dumpling; he had eyes as empty as the North Sea; he had several brown-paper parcels which he was quite incapable of collecting . . He had a large, shabby umbrella, which constantly fell on the floor. He did not seem to know which was the right end of his return ticket. He explained with a moon-calf simplicity to everybody in the carriage that he had to be careful, because he had something made of real silver 'with blue stones' in one of his brown-paper parcels. His quaint blending of Essex flatness with saintly simplicity continuously amused the Frenchman till the priest arrived (somehow) at Stratford with all his parcels, and came back for his umbrella.

After Sherlock Holmes, the next major metamorphosis of Dupin thus emerged with Chesterton's Father Brown in *The Blue Cross* (included in *The Innocence of Father Brown*, 1911).

Chesterton allows his readers to feel, at first, on more or less familiar ground, as the debts to the now-lengthening tradition are registered, even if a certain shift is already visible:

> The most incredible thing about miracles is that they happen . . there is in life an element of elfin coincidence which people reckoning on the prosaic may perpetually miss. As it has been well expressed in the paradox of Poe, wisdom should reckon on the unforeseen.

The due acknowledgement to Poe is made, with a certain grace and generosity, but Poe would not have been wholly happy with that term 'miracle' for his 'coincidences'. For Poe, any 'thrilling half-credence in the supernatural' prompted by 'coincidences of so seemingly marvellous a character' should quickly be quenched by studying the

Calculus of Probabilities and acknowledging the abstract majesty of mathematics.

And neither Edgar Allen Poe nor Sir Arthur Conan Doyle would have entirely approved of the next paragraphs:

> Aristide Valentin was unfathomably French; and the French intelligence is intelligence specially and solely. He was not 'a thinking machine'; for that is a brainless phrase of modem fatalism and materialism. A machine only is a machine because it cannot think. But he was a thinking man, and a plain man at the same time. All his wonderful successes, that looked like conjuring, had been gained by plodding logic, by clear and commonplace French thought. The French electrify the world not by starting any paradox, they electrify it by carrying out a truism. They carry a truism so far—as in the French Revolution. But exactly because Valentin understood reason, he understood the limits of reason. Only a man who knows nothing of motors talks of motoring without petrol; only a man who knows nothing of reason talks of reasoning without strong, undisputed first principles. Here he had no strong first principles. Flambeau had been missed at Harwich; and if he was in London at all, he might be anything from a tall tramp on Wimbledon Common to a tall toastmaster at the Hotel Metropole. In such a naked state of nescience, Valentin had a view and a method of his own.
>
> In such cases he reckoned on the unforeseen. In such cases, when he could not follow the train of the reasonable, he coldly and carefully followed the train of the unreasonable. Instead of going to the right places banks, police stations, rendezvous—he systematically went to the wrong places; knocked at every empty house, turned down every cul de sac, went up every lane blocked with rubbish, went round every crescent that led him uselessly out of the way. He defended this crazy course quite logically. He said that if one had a clue this was the worst way; but if one had no clue at all it was the best, because there was just the chance that any

> oddity that caught the eye of the pursuer might be the same that had caught the eye of the pursued. Somewhere a man must begin, and it had better be just where another man might stop.

And even though Sherlock Holmes might, just once, have been beaten by an ex-opera singer's 'wit', he would be unlikely to endorse Valentin's general philosophy of criminal composition:

> 'The criminal is the creative artist; the detective only the critic,' he said with a sour smile, and lifted his coffee cup to his lips slowly, and put it down very quickly. He had put salt in it.

Already in these first few pages of the tale, Chesterton has introduced a number of the variations that could occupy our attention in any study of the tradition from now on—not least of which ought to be the lacing of the detective-story with humour, from the whimsical to the wise-cracking to the metaphysically witty.

The bumbling Father Brown clearly shares some of the traits of his predecessors: he, too, is an unofficial amateur, though equipped with a surprising omnipresence and sometimes bizarrely appropriate knowledge; he too is celibate and apparently a-sexual; he too indulges, in this tale, in at least quasi-criminal actions, and he too seems to rely upon, and appeal to, a law which is superior to and can, if necessary, override the official law. But even in these characteristics Fr. Brown is significantly different from Dupin and Holmes. His knowledge of criminal skills is derived not from cold observation or from collected data, but from an apparently warm and friendly relation with his 'flock':

> 'How in Tartarus,' cried Flambeau, 'did you ever hear of the spiked bracelet?'
> 'Oh, one's little flock, you know!' said Father Brown, arching his eyebrows rather blankly. 'When I was a

> curate in Hartlepool, there were three of them with spiked bracelets.'

His celibacy is not for the sake of solitude or to keep pure his ratiocinative processes, but rather to accommodate a more comprehensive love—and when he does speak of 'the softer passions' it is not with 'a gibe and a sneer' (as Holmes did) but with delight and awesome wonder (as in *The Scandal of Father Brown* or *The Insoluble Problem*). His occasional misdemeanours are in a minor key, and mainly directed against property rather than people (a splash of soup on a wall, a delicately smashed window). And the law to which he has final recourse is a law of charity and forgiveness.

But it is the strategy of the tale itself that takes our analysis a step further. For we are positioned by this tale neither as admiring pawn (Holmes's Watson) nor as competitor (Poe's reader), but rather as alert and active follower. Our stand-in, Valentin, begins the chase from salt-cellar to high Hampstead Heath from sheer hunch; he follows not a chain of clues to be pieced together by reasoning but a succession of cues to be recognised, trusted in, and responded to. But the reader who merely follows unthinkingly, going along passively for an apparently interminable ride atop a crawling omnibus, until Valentin (inevitably) spots the next cue, is likely to kick him- or herself at the end for not bothering to grasp the double function of those cues: they both draw the detective after and confirm the criminal in advance—as Fr. Brown explains:

> 'A man generally makes a small scene if he finds salt in his coffee; if he doesn't, he has some reason for keeping quiet . . A man generally objects if his bill is three times too big. If he pays it, he has some motive for passing unnoticed.'

Of course, GKC, having pulled this extra rabbit out of a hat that seemed long emptied, leaves the reader with a faint worry as to whether Fr. Brown would care to justify all his other mildly outrageous acts as more than mere cues for Valentin.

Not that it seems to matter much; the fun is in the chase itself, and it doesn't even seem a cheat when, Holmes-like, the tale gives information and deduction together, and the first clue last ('that little bulge up your sleeve where you people have the spiked bracelet')—after all, the 'story' has to start somehow, and we knew whom we were chasing anyway, as soon as Valentin got off the boat: 'Flambeau was in England'. Nor does it seem to matter very much in which particular way Fr. Brown foils the attempted theft, nor even whether Flambeau is arrested or not at the end. In fact, most of the elements that hold our interest in Poe or in Conan Doyle seem only marginally relevant to this tale of a detective, a criminal, a crime (prevented) and a pursuit.

The comment that 'the criminal is the creative artist, the detective only the critic' provides the appropriate prompt. The interest of the tale, if it has one, lies, it seems, in its 'aesthetic' (or even Aestheticist) appeal—though its artistry may seem a touch artificial today; there is a somewhat Decadent dependence on insistent alliteration, a kind of fervour of 'fine' writing, an over-reliance on assonance and simile:

> Between the silver ribbon of morning and the green glittering ribbon of sea, the boat touched Harwich and let loose a swarm of folk like flies. . .

Such writing is rightly suspect, perhaps. But in Chesterton's slightly strained, though sometimes attractive, striving after 'effect', we should at least be prepared to recognise the precursor of some later developments in detective fiction: we don't read Pinget for the plot and we do indeed read Robbe-Grillet for the writing. But it's not only the writing, the pervasive and possibly irritating trickery of style, that is governed by 'aesthetic' considerations. If we react with any degree of pleasure to the list of Flambeau's 'crimes', for example, it's because they appeal to a certain kind of imaginative delight in the absurd or ludicrous: the child, or the anarchist, in us responds favourably to:

> how he turned the *juge d'instruction* upside down and stood him on his head, 'to clear his mind;' how he ran down the Rue de Rivoli with a policeman under each arm . . .

And some of us are prepared to suspend any rational objection when we read that:

> It was he who ran the great Tyrolean Dairy Company in London, with no dairies, no cows, no carts, no milk, but with some thousand subscribers. These he served by the simple operation of moving the little milk-cans outside people's doors to the doors of his own customers.

We might even feel that this particular example indicates a fairly acute grasp of some important principles of commerce.

In general, however, we are clearly in the same kind of world as that of a cartoon comedy, a two-dimensional and rather vividly-coloured fantasy, in which some of the things we might, in our more carefree moments, like to do ourselves can actually happen:

> 'Sorry to confuse your accounts, but it'll pay for the window.' 'What window?' I says. 'The one I'm going to break,' he says, and smashed that blessed pane with his umbrella.

When the sober British police inspector asks 'Are we after escaped lunatics?', he is almost on the right track; but the more appropriate term might be 'fools'.

The tale suggests a suspension of the ordinary rules of behaviour, a reversal of the everyday, which has affinities with that sacred suspension of power-relations known in mediaeval Europe as the Feast of Fools, when the first are put last and the weak have a crack at ruling the strong, when the lowest novice becomes the Lord Abbot and the Boy-Prince reigns. It's deeply appropriate that Fr. Brown should leave behind him a trail of reversals: salt swapped for sugar, tangerines labelled nuts and nuts labelled tangerines, a broken window paid for before it is broken, a parcel inquired for before it is lost, and a thief attempting to steal his own parcel. The Feast of Fools was indeed an escape, from hierarchy and oppression, but only a limited and temporary asylum, a merely momentary image of an impossible but promised Utopia. And Fr. Brown's antics too have their limits, though rather interesting ones.

Perhaps the only time the reader is offered a clue, on an equal footing with both Fr. Brown and the listening Valentin, is in the 'innocently clerical conversation' on the darkening heath—and Valentin, at least, misses the point:

> The taller priest nodded his bowed head and said: 'Ah, yes, these modem infidels appeal to their reason; but who can look at those millions of worlds and not feel that there may well be wonderful universes above us where reason is utterly unreasonable?'
>
> 'No,' said the other priest; 'reason is always reasonable, even in the last limbo, in the lost borderland of things. I know that people charge the Church with lowering reason but it is just the other way. Alone on earth, the Church makes reason really supreme. Alone on earth, the Church affirms that God Himself is bound by reason.'
>
> The other priest raised his austere face to the spangled sky and said: 'Yet who knows if in that infinite universe. . . ?'
>
> 'Only infinite physically,' said the little priest, turning sharply in his seat, 'not infinite in the sense of escaping from the laws of truth.'
>
> Valentin behind his tree was tearing his finger-nails with silent fury. He seemed almost to hear the sniggers of the English detectives whom he had brought so far on a fantastic guess only to listen to the metaphysical gossip of two mild old parsons.

As Fr. Brown is later to point out, Flambeau here gives away his disguise as a priest, since to attack reason is 'bad theology' (whatever your brand of 'theology' happens to be).

Unlike Poe's narrator, Fr. Brown would not agree that God, creator of the world, 'can, at will, control or modify it'. God, too, for Fr. Brown, is 'bound by reason', by the 'laws of truth'. The truth, even the most scandalous, can hold no terrors for God's undercover agents: 'Has it never struck you that a man who does next to nothing but hear men's real sins is not likely to be wholly unaware of human evil?' But then it becomes rather important to know what is comprised by 'reason', what is legislated for in those 'laws of truth'. Fr. Brown continues the argument:

> Reason and justice grip the remotest and the loneliest star. Look at those stars. Don't they look as if they were single diamonds and sapphires ? Well, you can imagine any mad botany or geology you please. Think of forests of adamant with leaves of brilliants. Think the moon is a blue moon, a single elephantine sapphire. But don't fancy that all that frantic astronomy would make the smallest difference to the reason and justice of conduct. On plains of opal, under cliffs cut out of pearl, you would still find a notice-board, 'Thou shalt not steal.'

It's an intriguing piece of rhetoric. It reverses (once more) familiar expectations, this time of 'science': that the world as scrutinised by physics and chemistry is universally shaped by the same basic principles, whereas norms of behaviour, rules of conduct and codes of morality, are relative, specific to the societies which generate and rely upon them. It is Flambeau who can conceive of quite different worlds, wonderfully alternative universes, but for Chesterton himself, Flambeau's creator, there is a rational limit to social experiment: 'The French electrify the world not by starting any paradox, they electrify it by carrying out a truism. They carry a truism so far—as in the French Revolution' —but no further. Even Proudhon's mildly paradoxical thought that property might be theft is beyond the ken of this 'reason'.

Of course, however, if there were neither property nor theft, there could be no detective story, even in fantastic vein, centred on the attempted theft of a cross 'made of real silver "with blue stones".' And with property, inevitably, goes not only theft but policemen: 'even as he turned away to collect his property, the three policemen came out from under the twilight trees'.

Yet Flambeau's gesture of greeting to Valentin at this climactic point reminds us once again that we do not take this story of crime and detection too seriously: 'Flambeau was an artist and a sportsman. He stepped back and swept Valentin a great bow'.

Crime, in this tale, is a game to play, a matter of art and sport: the law is necessary to the game not as its governing rules (to break the law is certainly not to 'cheat' in this game) nor is breaking the law the object, quite, of the game (the goal is the cross itself). The law has a rather curious status: it defines the character of some of the moves (some are within the law, others not), and it defines one of the teams (Valentin is, in colloquial parlance, 'the law'), but its main function is to get the game going, to say which team starts with the ball in the first place (as, in chess, it is always White who gets the first move). And just as the law acts as a necessary but curiously irrelevant premise to the play of the text, so it seems a necessary premise for the game of crime—yet one that must always have an air of artifice.

One has the constant impression that Chesterton's story could actually get along quite nicely even if there were no law, no crime, no punishment, no criminal, no policeman; the chase could always find some other object. Nevertheless the story, as written, relies upon the law: this story needs the law, even if it suggests some possible, wild reversal of the whole genre: a detective tale without a crime, a criminal, a detective or the police.

There is in fact a real paradox imaged in *The Blue Cross*. It is always possible to recognise both that 'the Law' is only constituted by particular laws and that those laws are created and enforced primarily to maintain and safeguard a particular distribution of power and of property which is arbitrary, in the sense that there can be no entirely rational justification for any specific differential allocation of power and privilege; any such rationales can always be challenged in the name of a different or 'higher' rationale. But then any system of law, not only all particular laws, can seem an arbitrary and unjustified encumbrance; one response to that realisation is then a more or less explicit wish for a society that could operate without 'law', an an-archy (literally, a society without a chief magistrate) where nobody 'reigns'. It is only in fantasy, by a suspension of the real, by the use of a playful and perhaps child-like imagination, that we can envisage such a Utopia. Yet it is perhaps partly by that constant recourse to 'dreams' in which not 'law' but art and game (which may have their own 'laws') provide the principles which shape society, that we can continue to affirm that: 'somewhere a man must begin, and it had better be just where another man might stop'.

The Utopian, anarchist tradition may at times be caricatured as limited to slightly lunatic gestures, like smashing windows or throwing soup at the wall, but without such hankerings after *bouleversement*, after a permanent festival of the oppressed, it is doubtful whether 'plodding logic [or] clear and common-sense French thought' will ever electrify the world.

What blocks the 'progress' of 'reason' is sometimes brute force—at the point where Fr. Brown resorts to his rhetorical defence of universal reason, Flambeau 'without changing by the faintest shade his attitude or voice' simply says 'Just hand over that sapphire cross of yours, will you? We're all alone here, and I could pull you to pieces like a rag doll.' But at other times it is the elaborations of 'reason' itself that drive the reasoner into an impasse. Chesterton has two interesting remarks in an essay of 1908 entitled *Orthodoxy*:

> Everyone who has had the misfortune to talk with people in the heart or on the edge of mental disorder, knows that their most sinister quality is a horrible clarity of detail; a connecting of one thing with another in a map more elaborate than a maze.

and:

> Imagination does not breed insanity. Exactly what does breed insanity is reason. Poets do not go mad; but chess-players do. Mathematicians go mad, and cashiers; but creative artists very seldom. I am not, as will be seen, in any sense attacking logic: I only say that this

> danger does lie in logic, not in imagination. Artistic paternity is as wholesome as physical paternity. Moreover, it is worthy of remark that when a poet really was morbid it was commonly because he had some weak spot of rationality on his brain. Poe, for instance, really was morbid; not because he was poetical, but because he was specially analytical. Even chess was too poetical for him; he disliked chess because it was full of knights and castles, like a poem. He avowedly preferred the black discs of draughts, because they were more like the mere black dots on a diagram.

The reference to Poe's preference for draughts is to the opening of *The Murders in the Rue Morgue*, and we might easily return here to that famous opening. But let me move in a different direction instead.

Paul Feyerabend opens his *Against Method: outline of an anarchist theory of knowledge* thus:

> The following essay is written in the conviction that anarchism, while perhaps not the most attractive political philosophy, is certainly excellent medicine for epistemology, and for the philosophy of science. The reason is not difficult to find.
>
> 'History generally, and the history of revolutions in particular, is always richer in content, more varied, more many-sided, more lively and subtle than even the best' historian and the best methodologist can imagine. History is full of 'accidents and conjunctures and curious juxtapositions of events' and it demonstrates to us the 'complexity of human change and the unpredictable character of the ultimate consequences of any given act or decision of men'. Are we really to believe that the naive and simple-minded rules which methodologists take as their guide are capable of accounting for such a 'maze of interactions'? And is it not clear that successful participation in a process of this kind is possible only for a ruthless opportunist who is not tied to any particular philosophy and who adopts whatever procedure seems to fit the occasion?

Feyerabend's first quotation in that passage is from V. I. Lenin, *Left-Wing Communism—an infantile disorder* (1920), and it is worth giving a bit more from that polemical pamphlet of Lenin:

> History as a whole, and the history of revolutions in particular, is always richer in content, more varied, more multiform, more lively and ingenious than is imagined by even the best parties, the most class-conscious vanguards of the most advanced classes.
> This can readily be understood, because even the finest of vanguards express the class-consciousness, will, passion and imagination of tens of thousands, whereas at moments of great upsurge and the exertion of all human capacities, revolutions are made by the class-consciousness, will, passion and imagination of tens of millions, spurred on by a most acute struggle of classes.
> Two very important practical conclusions follow from this: first, that in order to accomplish its task the revolutionary class must be able to master all forms or aspects of social activity without exception (completing after the capture of political power—sometimes at great risk and with very great danger—what it did not complete before the capture of power); second, that the revolutionary class must be prepared for the most rapid and brusque replacement of one form by another.

Feyerabend continues to interweave Lenin and a transposition of Lenin in 'quoting' this passage:

> First, that in order to fulfil its task, the revolutionary class [i.e. the class of those who want to change either a part of society such as science, or society as a whole] must be able to master all forms or aspects of social activity without exception [it must be able to understand, and apply, not only one particular methodology, but any methodology, and any variation thereof it can imagine] . . . .

Lenin himself goes on to discuss the need for both 'legal' and 'illegal' revolutionary work, for work even in 'non-revolutionary bodies':

> Inexperienced revolutionaries often think that legal methods of struggle are opportunist because, in this field, the bourgeoisie has most frequently deceived and duped the workers (particularly in 'peaceful' and non-revolutionary times), while illegal methods of struggle are revolutionary. That, however, is wrong. The truth is that those parties and leaders are opportunists and traitors to the working class that are unable or unwilling (do not say, 'I can't'; say, 'I shan't') to use illegal methods of struggle in conditions such as those which prevailed, for example, during the imperialist war of 1914—18, when the bourgeoisie of the freest democratic countries most brazenly and brutally deceived the workers, and smothered the truth about the predatory character of the war. But revolutionaries who are incapable of combining illegal forms of struggle with every form of legal struggle are poor revolutionaries indeed. It is not difficult to be a revolutionary when revolution has already broken out and is in spate, when all people are joining the revolution just because they are carried away, because it is the vogue, and sometimes even from careerist motives. After its victory, the proletariat has to make the most strenuous efforts, even the most painful, so as to 'liberate' itself from such pseudo-revolutionaries. It is far more difficult—and far more precious —to be a revolutionary when the conditions for direct, open, really mass and really revolutionary struggle do not yet exist, to be able to champion the interests of the revolution (by propaganda, agitation and organisation) in non-revolutionary bodies, and quite often in downright reactionary bodies, in a non-revolutionary situation, among the masses who are incapable of immediately appreciating the need for revolutionary methods of action.

Lenin then cites Britain as an example of where 'no one can tell in advance how soon a real proletarian revolution will flare up . . and what immediate cause will most serve to rouse, kindle and impel into the struggle the very wide masses, who are still dormant . . It is possible that the breach will be forced, the ice broken, by a parliamentary crisis, or by a crisis arising from colonial and imperialist contradictions, which are hopelessly entangled and are becoming increasingly painful and acute.' Quite rightly, Lenin does not speculate further.

It is a familiar story that Lenin gave up playing chess, as too much of a distraction from the tasks of revolution. It's also a familiar fantasy that when living in Zurich in 1916-17, on the eve of the actual but unexpected revolution, Lenin may have been writing his *Imperialism: the highest stage of capitalism* across a library-table from James Joyce, then completing *Ulysses*, while the two of them might even have dropped into the Cafe Voltaire to see what those anarchist artists Tzara and Ball were up to. Such a marvellous coincidence as Lenin's flat being just across the street from the home of Dada was bound to attract an author of travesties.

But it is even more provoking of wild laughter that the latest twist in that supremely meta-methodological discipline, the philosophy of science, should have produced a self-declared Dadaist (see Feyerabend's footnote to his use of 'anarchist' in his sub-title—a footnote to a title-page being a pleasantly Dadaist gesture).

Perhaps the reason for that declaration of Dadaism is ultimately to be located in that curiously persistent problem of bonding 'data' and 'hypothesis': either the one is already shaped inextricably by the other or an unbridgeable 'gap' erupts 'between' them. And one curiously persistent feature of models of 'revolution' derived from the Bolshevik moment of 1917 is that they seem to require a moment of absolute 'rupture', a sudden and total break in the familiar chains that bind the future to the past (such a 'rupture' could only be recognised or validated as a 'revolution' retrospectively). Those who back away from 'anarchy' may have to permanently postpone such a revolution.

It's an intriguing and rather pleasantly fantastic thought that at some particular moment the *juge d'instruction* should have to be, very suddenly and perhaps very sharply, turned upside down and stood on his head 'to clear his mind'—or change it. Such a 'crime' might indeed be an image of a non-ordinary law, a paradigm of the politics of the extra-ordinary, an echo and anticipation of the Festival of the oppressed.

*

Q. 6 RAYMOND CHANDLER, *The Big Sleep*

In October 1949 Raymond Chandler, in a letter to James Sandoe, complained:[1]

> As for mysteries, that's hopeless. There don't seem to be any worth the trouble [of reading]. It would be an excellent thing right now if someone would come along with a good cool analytical mystery, the hell with suspense and witty dialogue, and let us look at the fundamentals for fresh. The whole form has lost its way, the emphasis has gone to inessential matters.

The same year, in *Casual Notes on the Mystery Novel*, Chandler re-stated some of the 'fundamentals' of the genre:

> The mystery must elude a reasonably intelligent reader. This, and the problem of honesty, are the two most baffling elements in mystery writing. Some of the best detective stories ever written do not elude an intelligent reader to the end . . But it is one thing to guess the murderer and quite another to be able to justify the guess by reasoning.

Chandler was very much concerned with the problem of what he calls 'honesty' in constructing the tale: the reader must be given 'the sort of facts which can be reasoned from', and must have a fair chance of making the right inferences. But two comments in this connection are worth linking:

> Inferences from the facts are the detective's stock in trade, but he should disclose enough of his thinking to keep the reader's mind thinking along with him.

---

[1] For this and subsequent quotations see *Raymond Chandler Speaking*, ed. D. Gardiner & K. Sorley Walker, London, 1961.

> There must come a time when the detective has made up his mind and has not given the reader this bit of news, a point as it were (and many old hands recognise it without much difficulty) when the detective suddenly stops thinking out loud and ever so gently closes the door of his mind in the reader's face.

But, as has been clear since the days of Poe's Dupin, there is a sense in which the detective cannot disclose his 'thinking', but only the results of that thinking. He may register that curious moment of insight for the reader but only retrospectively can he offer an account of it. (Fielding's send-up of *Pamela* in his *Shamela* might be recalled at this point.)

There is a clear moment of insight in Chandler's novel of 1940, *Farewell, My Lovely*:

> I nodded across the office at Mr. Rembrandt, then I reached for my hat and went out. I was half-way to the elevator before the thought hit me. It hit me without any reason or sense, like a dropped brick. I stopped and leaned against the marbled wall and pushed my hat around on my head and suddenly I laughed. (chapter 15)

The same thought may have struck the reader long before (that Marriott got Marlowe's card from Mrs Florian), but until it strikes Marlowe the reader can't take the next step—only Marlowe can pick up a phone and confirm the link between Marriott and Mrs Florian. The reader is always, sometimes irritatingly, dependent upon the detective's reasoning and the 'disclosure' can't, unfortunately, be mutual.

The problem is, in other words, not so much that the reader guesses while the detective 'reasons' but that the reader has no way of shaping events in order to 'test' a guess that presents itself without 'any reason or sense'; the reader can't prompt the detective. Which is one further reason why Chandler was correct to comment, in 1940, a propos of Agatha Christie's *Ten Little Niggers*: (*sic*)

> I'm very glad I read the book because it finally and for all time settled a question in my mind that had at least some lingering doubt attached to it. Whether it is possible to write a strictly honest mystery of the classic type. It isn't. To get the complication you fake the clues, the timing, the play of coincidence, assume certainties where only 50 per cent chances exist at most. To get the surprise murderer you fake the character, which hits me hardest of all, because I have a sense of character.

It's not surprising to find Chandler, after this comment, remarking in 1944 that 'I really don't seem to take the mystery element in the detective story as seriously as I should', or, in the same year, that 'the detective or mystery story as an art-form has been so thoroughly explored that the real problem for a writer now is to avoid writing a mystery story while appearing to do so'.

In 1947 he seems to have considered a new twist in the tradition: 'No, I am not working on a story of murder without detection. I have such a story in mind, but have not got down to it yet', and in 1949 he was still hankering after a development in the genre that would not 'fake the character' but would rather 'fake' being a 'mystery' at all:

> I am not satisfied that the thing can't be done, nor that sometime, somewhere, perhaps not now or by me, a novel cannot be written which, ostensibly a mystery and keeping the spice of mystery, will actually be a novel of character and atmosphere with an over-tone of violence and fear.

ii

A decade earlier Chandler had already written about *The Big Sleep*, his first novel, published in 1939, in similar terms:

> I was . . intrigued by a situation where the mystery is solved more by the exposition and understanding of a single character, always well in evidence, than by the

> slow and sometimes long-winded concatenation of circumstances.

Dupin had, long before, relied upon a similar 'fathoming of character', albeit marginally. In *The Big Sleep* such 'fathoming' is not difficult: from the very first chapter the (nympho-) mania of Miss Carmen Sternwood is apparent to all but the dimmest. But the strategy of the text is then to lead us into a tangle of ramifications, elaborations, and mystifications, weaving together in a complex pattern a pornography racket, a blackmail racket, a gambling racket, police corruption, homosexuality and an assortment of violent deaths (Geiger, Brody, Owen, Jones, Canino).

The thread we are ostensibly following through this maze derives from a possibly blameless request that some gambling debts, though 'legally uncollectable', should be honoured. But it is hardly 'deduction' or 'inference from the facts' that keeps Marlowe in touch thereafter with the varied goings-on. Coincidences of timing, chance encounters, and some implausible luck keep the story moving, and the reader tails along, waiting, like Chesterton's Valentin, to see what bizarre incident will happen next.

Within that general play of 'collateral' events, Marlowe does do some clearing of the 'fog' by putting twos and twos together, but his main weapon is a fast tongue rather than a scientific calculus: the set-pieces of the book are conversational sparring matches in which the object is to trick the interlocutor, either into divulging information that could have been kept concealed or into being misled by varieties of verbal deception; and, occasionally, a gun can enforce a degree of suitable loquacity.

But does it matter, in the end, whether all the loose-ends in this by-play are tied neatly into a final bow? In 1949 Chandler wrote:

> I remember several years ago when Howard Hawks was making *The Big Sleep*, the movie, he and Bogart got into an argument as to whether one of the characters was murdered or committed suicide. They sent me a wire asking me, and dammit I didn't know either.

That such a question can remain unanswered in the novel indicates one function of the complex 'plotting' that occupies most of the book: it serves to distract the reader from concentrating on the 'real' question which structures the quest—'who killed Rusty Regan?' But that is only the 'real' question in the sense that to answer it is to finish the novel; once that hidden (yet insistently raised and repressed) enigma is resolved the story is over.

Yet, in principle, the alert reader could ask that question by chapter 2, guess the answer by chapter 3, and be able to 'justify' it by, at the latest, chapter 24 (the incident with the naked Carmen that clinches Marlowe's account in the final chapter). But were the novel, or Marlowe, or the reader, to arrive at 'the answer' by chapter 24, the novel would nevertheless not have 'finished', since much of the collateral 'plot' is still only half-unfolded. And, equally, 'solving' the various subordinate mysteries in no important way contributes directly to arriving at the solution to Regan's disappearance.

The 'answer' given in the last chapter is not, therefore, either the final step in a chain of deductions (clues) nor the last in a causally connected sequence of events (cues); the story is finally given shape not so much by a 'solution' of its 'problem' as by a 'resolution' of its 'suspense': the pattern of expectation is not so much 'where does that clue lead?' but simply 'what is going to happen next?' (which partly accounts for the sense of awkward 'second start' in chapter 20)—and the logic of such suspense leads simply to the continual question 'how is it going to end?' And we know the answer to that question only when it ends.

But whereas a solution to a problem can be correct or incorrect, an 'ending' can only be 'satisfactory' or 'unsatisfactory'. Our criteria for judging the shape of this tale are, necessarily, 'aesthetic'. The structure of Chandler's novel offers another variation on the data-hypothesis bond: we accept the 'relevance' of so much that is 'marginal' in the book insofar as we are satisfied by the totality; we retrospectively allow the 'collateral' insofar as we are convinced by the 'whole'. But that is primarily a matter of the effect of 'closure' achieved by the final pages, even by the final sentence: 'I never saw her again'—the whole story, with all its still trailing elements, is signalled as conclusively over, done with.

With Chandler, the detective story aims for the 'organic', for the 'form' of 'good fiction':

> The mystery novel must have a sound story value apart from the mystery element. The idea is revolutionary to some of the classicists and most distasteful to all second-rate performers. Never-theless it is sound. All really good mysteries are re-read, some of them many times. Obviously this would not happen if the puzzle were the only motive for the reader's interest. The mysteries that survive over the years invariably have the qualities of good fiction.

Another note elaborates one aspect of this position:

> The mystery novel must punish the criminal in one way or another, not necessarily by operation of the law courts. Contrary to popular belief, this has nothing to do with morality. It is part of the logic of the form. Without this the story is like an unresolved chord in music. It leaves a sense of irritation.

It then surely follows that the form of punishment has also to be appropriate, part of the overall pattern. Yet at the end of *The Big Sleep* Miss Carmen Sternwood is not, in any normal sense, 'punished'. Part of the reason is that she herself is 'not normal' (ch.22). Since the tale revolves round the 'exposition and understanding of a single character', it is perhaps not surprising that the 'ending' should be 'appropriate' to the character involved. But might not some readers, at least, be rather irritated at this somewhat lop-sided 'resolution', at the thought of Rusty Regan's murderess being merely 'taken away' to be 'cured', privately and unofficially, while another murderer, the homosexual Carol Lundgren, is given no such chance.

iii

The problem at this point could be posed in more general terms. Even if a rational chain of detection, from facts to inference, from crime to criminal, could be constructed, could that chain be extended to embrace the specific 'punishment' that follows? Should, for example, the punishment fit the crime or fit the (character of the) criminal? Or is 'punishment' itself an 'inappropriate' term? And how do we decide?

One aspect of that general problem was explored by Max Weber in his analysis of bureaucracy:[2]

> The more complicated and specialized modem culture becomes, the more its external supporting apparatus demands the personally detached and strictly 'objective' expert, in lieu of the master of older social structures, who was moved by personal sympathy and favor, by grace and gratitude. . . As a rule, only bureaucracy has established the foundation for the administration of a rational law conceptually systematized . . .
>
> The 'rational' interpretation of law on the basis of strictly formal conceptions stands opposite the kind of adjudication that is primarily bound to sacred traditions. The single case that cannot be unambiguously decided by tradition is either settled by concrete 'revelation' (oracle, prophetic dicta, or ordeal—that is, by 'charismatic' justice) or by informal judgments rendered in terms of concrete ethical or other practical valuations. This is 'Kadi-justice', as R. Schmidt has fittingly called it. Or, formal judgments are rendered, though not by subsumption under rational concepts, but by drawing on 'analogies' and by depending upon and interpreting concrete 'precedents'. This is 'empirical justice'.

---

[2] *From Max Weber*, ed. H. H. Gerth & C. Wright Mills, London 1948, p. 216. (Cited hereafter as *W*.)

The 'ideal type' of judge within a bureaucratic, rational, formal legal system can be described in a way that echoes Watson's description, in *A Scandal in Bohemia*, of Sherlock Holmes as a perfect reasoning machine with none of the softer passions:

> The conception of the modem judge as an automaton into which the files and the costs are thrown in order that it may spill forth the verdict at the bottom along with the reasons, read mechanically from codified paragraphs—this conception is angrily rejected, perhaps because a certain approximation to this type is implied by a consistent bureaucratization of justice. (*W*, p.219)

'In principle', indeed, 'the idea of "a law without gaps" is vigorously disputed', writes Weber; but if there are indeed 'gaps' does that not undermine the whole 'principle' of a rigorously rational system? And how are they to be 'filled'? Could one have a blending of 'rational law' with 'Kadi-justice' or with 'empirical justice'? But if Kadi-justice appeals to 'revelation', what is the source of that 'revelation'? And what is the 'empirical' basis of 'empirical justice'?

One suggestion might be that both Kadi and empirical justice implicitly appeal to 'Literature', to sacred texts and even, more or less directly, to 'fiction'. (An essay by Roland Barthes, *Dominici, or the triumph of Literature*, in his *Mythologies*, explores this possibility in relation to legal judgements in modem France.) If therefore we now explore 'rational law' we may in fact find ourselves back with the other brands.

Weber writes:

> The only decisive point . . is that in principle a system of rationally debatable "reasons" stands behind every act of bureaucratic administration, that is, either subsumption under norms or a weighing of ends and means. (*W*, p. 220)

But whose 'norms' and whose 'ends'? (In *The Big Sleep* Carmen is 'not normal'—but according to what norm?)

The question of the 'norms' which underpin and justify a whole system of law has been explored by the 'critical criminologists'. The logic of their case is that legal 'norms' have to be situated within a total context, that what is required is a 'fully social theory' which can embrace not only 'the political economy of crime' but also 'the political economy, the social psychology and the social dynamics of social reaction to deviance'.[3] Nothing less, in fact, than a total theory of society is required. (It is interesting that at this point in their argument they refer to the work of a novelist as the best-available instantiation of such a 'total theory': see *NC*, pp. 277-8.)

Such an account is also required, logically, by any application of law which seeks to take notice of all the 'individual circumstances' of a case, or fully to take cognisance of the 'character' of the accused—if, as Dupin pointed out, 'it is the malpractice of the courts to confine evidence and discussion to the bounds of apparent relevancy', any court which seeks to extend the area of 'relevance' beyond the 'recognised and booked principles' of evidence, can have no fully rational grounds for setting new bounds. On the other hand, if the notion of 'norms' is itself driven back through the hierarchy of bureaucratic 'means and ends', the only 'logical' stopping place tends to be that mysterious 'reason' known as '*raison d'etat*', which perhaps is not so very different from the 'revelations' of Kadi-justice: 'oracle, prophetic dicta or ordeal'.

Foucault's work on the history of crime and punishment[4] suggested one 'solution', in principle, to this 'anomaly of the most rigidly exact . . applied to . . the most intangible in speculation' (to adapt Dupin): what he calls 'the normalisation of the power of normalisation'. The logic he traces is that if the 'criminal' does not act in accordance with the 'norm' or, to put it more generally, is 'not normal', the

---

[3] *The New Criminology*, by I. Taylor, P. Walton & J. Young, London 1973, p. 276. Cited hereafter as *NC*).

[4] M. Foucault, *Discipline and Punish*, London 1977, especially Part 4. Hereafter *DP*.

'humane' form of eradication is to 'normalise' him, by punishment, coercion, imprisonment, re-training, psychological re-adjustment, re-education, or whatever means will achieve that end. But if some methods have proved successful in normalising the criminal *after* his crime and capture, would it not be more sensible to apply those methods *in advance* to potential criminals? And since no one can be sure who is a potential criminal until a crime has actually been committed, and even then there is no guarantee that the real culprit will be detected, the logic of this solution is to extend normalisation techniques developed for 'criminals' to everyone. That way crime might be finally eradicated—and, with it, the need for law: the dream of anarchy would be finally realised! (At the same time, however, such an extension of normalisation techniques might logically have a tendency, if successful, to create more deviants—since the 'bounds' of the 'normal' would tend to encroach more and more upon previously 'collateral' matters.)

Foucault locates the linchpin of what he calls the 'carceral texture of society' in the 'model prison'. In its combination of total surveillance and 'scientific' human micro-engineering the ideal prison of the humane reformers has indeed threatened to become the model for a whole society—though eventually, perhaps, and for that very reason, a rather redundant model:

> now, as medicine, psychology, education, public assistance, 'social work' assume an ever greater share of the powers of supervision and assessment, the penal apparatus will be able, in turn, to become medicalised, psychologised, educationalised; and by the same token that turning-point represented by the prison becomes less useful when, through the gap between its penitentiary discourse and its effect of consolidating delinquency, it articulates the penal power and the disciplinary power. In the midst of all these mechanisms of normalisation, which are becoming ever more rigorous in their application, the specificity of the prison

> and its role as link are losing something of their purpose. (*DP*, p.306)

Perhaps Carol Lundgren, in a more enlightened and humane text, would indeed have also been sent to be 'cured' as simply 'not normal'—perhaps even before his crime.

The real problem remains, of course, even with this 'solution' of an extensive normalisation apparatuses: what is to count as 'the norm'? Weber pointed to one awkward facet of this problem:

> The propertyless masses especially are not served by a formal 'equality before the law' and a 'calculable' adjudication and administration, as demanded by 'bourgeois' interests. Naturally, in their eyes justice and administration should serve to compensate for their economic and social life-opportunities in the face of the propertied classes. Justice and administration can fulfil this function only if they assume an informal character to a far-reaching extent. It must be informal because it is substantively 'ethical' ('Kadi-justice'). Every sort of 'popular justice'—which usually does not ask for reasons and norms—as well as every sort of intensive influence on the administration by so-called public opinion, crosses the rational course of justice and administration just as strongly, and under certain conditions far more so, as the 'star chamber' proceedings of an 'absolute' ruler has been able to do. In this connection, that is, under the conditions of mass democracy, public opinion is communal conduct born of irrational 'sentiments'. Normally it is staged or directed by party leaders and the press. (*W*, p.221)

iv

If we now ask 'what is the norm?' in the text of *The Big Sleep*, the obvious answer has to be that Marlowe himself is: not a formulaic norm which might be rationally challenged or reformulated, but rather a living norm which is 'attractive' or 'sympathetic' to the reader; it is Marlowe's character which seems to offer us access to the undeclared norms that govern this book. (Poe, interestingly, wrote: 'the depicting of [Dupin's] character constituted my design.') But Marlowe's 'character' is by no means presented to us as 'normal': Marlowe is curiously unmotivated by those 'normal' passions of sex (like his predecessors—note the attitude behind the comment 'I'm unmarried because I don't like policemen's wives') and of money:

> I am so money greedy that for twenty-five bucks a day and expenses, mostly gasolene and whisky, I do my thinking myself, what there is of it; I risk my whole future, the hatred of the cops and of Eddie Mars and his pals, I dodge bullets and eat saps, and say thank you very much, if you have any more trouble, I hope you'll think of me, I'll just leave one of my cards in case anything comes up. I do all this for twenty-five bucks a day—and maybe just a little to protect what little pride a broken and sick old man has left in his blood...
>
> *The Big Sleep*, ch. 32. (Hereafter: *BS*)

It's worth elaborating for a moment Marlowe's relation to money. The plot 'begins' with Marlowe 'calling on four million dollars' and with him investigating a possible blackmail attempt; the final chapter sees Marlowe himself accused of wanting to blackmail those same millions—'I suppose you want money,' says Mrs Regan. But Marlowe, without even the motive of blackmail, keeps quiet about Carmen's murdering Regan and by his silence bends the law himself. His relation to money is indeed in parallel to his relation to the law: unlike both, say, Eddie Mars (whose wealth is basically 'illegitimate') and General Sternwood (whose wealth is basically 'legitimate'), Marlowe makes his living by a legitimate activity that yet operates askew to the law, in both senses: he is not part of the organised forces of 'law and order' (see his own comments on the Missing Persons Bureau, for example), though neither is he involved in organised crime. His 'crimes' arise from operating outside the rules of organised law-enforcement (see for example ch. 18), just as his self-employment is a way of avoiding the constraints of an 'organised' job (he was fired for insubordination).

In many respects, then, Marlowe slides between familiar pigeon-holes; the exchange between Marlowe and Mrs Regan suggests the basic ambivalence:

> You think he sent that loogan after you?
> What's a loogan?
> A guy with a gun.
> Are you a loogan?
> Sure, I laughed. But strictly speaking a loogan is on the wrong side of the fence.
> I often wonder if there is a wrong side.
> We're losing the subject.
> (*BS*, ch. 23)

If we now go back to the more general subject of 'norms' and 'law', it may be possible to locate these features of Marlowe's 'abnormal' character and position within a wider framework.

V

Jurgen Habermas[5] has suggested a different 'solution' to the problem of 'validating' a basic 'norm' in society. He argues that the liberal-capitalist state was able to appeal not to a transcendent or revealed norm nor to an arbitrary *raison d'etat*, but to a 'self-evident' norm embedded in its economic organisation:

> Bourgeois ideologies can assume a universalistic structure and appeal to generalisable interests because the property order has shed its political form and been converted into a relation of production that, it seems, can legitimate itself. The institution of the market can be founded on the justice inherent in the exchange of equivalents; and, for this reason, the bourgeois

---

[5] See his *Legitimation Crisis*, London 1976. (Cited hereafter as *LC*).

> constitutional state finds its justification in the legitimate relations of production. This is the message of rational natural law since Locke. The relations of production can do without a traditional authority legitimated from above. (*LC*, p. 22)

But then Marx's analysis of this alleged 'exchange of equivalents' struck a double-blow at bourgeois ideology:

> In Marx, therefore, theoretical analysis of the value form has the double task of uncovering both the steering principle of commerce in a market economy and the basic ideology of bourgeois class society. The theory of value serves, at the same time, the functional analysis of the economic system and the critique of ideology of a class domination that can be unmasked, even for the bourgeois consciousness, through the proof that in the labour market equivalents are not exchanged. (*LC*, p. 26)

In late capitalism, however, with the growing control of the 'market' by monopolistic company decisions and with the increasingly open contribution of the State to the maintenance and reproduction of the 'relations of production', the 'self-legitimation' of the market has ceased to be viable even in the eyes of its exponents; once again there is a need for explicitly political articulation and justification of 'ends and means'.

But the relatively simple contrast, as formul-ated by Weber, between 'the propertyless masses' and the 'propertied classes' is complicated by the effects of State intervention and by a differential relation of workers to employers, particularly in the area of the monopolies. Habermas summarises some of these complications thus:

> During the sixties, various authors, using the United States as an example, developed a three-sector model based on the distinction between the private and the public sectors. According to the model, private production is market-oriented, one sub-sector still being

> regulated by competition while the other is determined by the market strategies of oligopolies that tolerate a 'competitive fringe'. By contrast, in the public sector, especially in the armaments and space-travel industries, huge concerns have arisen whose investment decisions can be made almost without regard for the market . . . In the monopolistic and the public sectors, capital-intensive industries predominate; in the competitive sector, labor-intensive industries predominate. In the monopolistic and public sectors, companies are faced with strong unions. In the competitive sector workers are less well organised, and wage levels are correspondingly different. (*LC*, p. 54)

The combined effect of strong unions in certain sectors, the relative independence from market constraints of monopoly companies, and the politically-guided interventions of the State, is that in some sectors and for some workers the liberal-capitalist thesis of 'exchange of equivalents' is no longer operative, and—it is implied—the Marxist analysis of 'the value form' therefore no longer strictly obtains:

> 'Price setting', which replaces price competition in the oligopolistic markets, has its counterpart in the labour market. Just as the great concerns quasi-administratively control price movements in their markets, so too, on the other side, they obtain quasi-political compromises with union adversaries on wage movements. In those branches of industry belonging to the monopolistic and the public sectors, which are central to economic development, the commodity called labour power receives a 'political price'. The 'wage-scale partners' find a broad zone of compromise, since increased labour costs can be passed on through prices and since there is a convergence of the middle-range demands of both sides on the state—demands that aim at increasing productivity, qualifying labour power, and improving the social condition of the workers. The monopolistic sector can, as it were, externalise class conflict. (*LC*, p. 38)

There are, however, two distinct ways of perceiving these 'changes'. One, which might be economically appropriate to some sections of the population still operating in the 'competitive fringe' or outside of any organised employment at all, would be to see both the 'control' of the monopolies and the 'quasi-political compromises' effected by strong unions as forms of 'blackmail' against them; the rhetorical vocabulary is familiar, and is activated in editorials and press reports ('public opinion') whenever there is a major strike in an important industry: 'Blackmailing the community', 'Holding the Country to Ransom', etc. In such formulations the 'victims' of the 'blackmail' are alleged to be everyone, including 'the State', the monopolies and even those other trade unionists who happen not to be on strike themselves at that particular moment. In Britain, the 1974 miners' strike and the consequent General Election made the logic of this perspective clear, in the rhetorical question: 'Who Governs?'

But that question is in any case the question underpinning any discussion of *raison d'etat*, of social 'ends and means', of fundamental legal 'norms'. The alternative way of perceiving a situation of 'quasi-political compromise' involving monopolies, unions and government, could also be formulated in terms of 'blackmail': that the price of the unions' silence on more fundamental issues (including who actually does govern) is a relatively privileged 'political price' for some workers' labour power, at the expense perhaps of other workers, those in less organised areas and in sectors (or countries) which are difficult to unionise or less likely to be the beneficiaries of State intervention. Crucially, such 'compromises' may serve as a substitute for any fundamental shift in or challenge to the continuing power of the monopolies, including their power over State interventions and 'government'. The logic of this perspective would perhaps be embodied in the often not-so-rhetorical question: 'Who are the class traitors?'

It would be possible to discuss at least some aspects of this analysis of late capitalism in terms of structural parallels within *The Big Sleep*. For example, the position Marlowe occupies *vis-á-vis* the other main protagonists in the plot is somewhat parallel to the position that might be felt to be their own by someone who regarded both the unions and the large capitalist companies as tarred with the same brush, as operating 'legally' but 'illegitimately': the difference between Eddie Mars and General Sternwood would then be seen as a matter of degree, even though Sternwood is much the more 'respectable'.

Equally, the official forces of law and order (the State apparatuses) would then be regarded as at best incompetent, almost certainly hand-in-glove with those they are supposed to control, and at worst corrupted and controlled themselves. What is then seen as needed in such a situation is precisely for someone (a Marlowe) to 'take the law into their own hands'. Thus one could fairly easily outline a case for regarding Marlowe's ambivalent attitudes as reproducing in large part the dilemmas and reactions of a traditional stereotype of the petty bourgeois proto-fascist.

Equally, however, and quite differently, one could regard Marlowe's final option of 'silence' as echoing the 'political compromise' of the 'reformist' within a system which is rejected at one level of response but basically endorsed, perhaps rather cynically admired, and ultimately is even protected at another level.

And one could also sketch another alternative interpretation which would place Marlowe as a conservative moralist marooned ineffectually, for the most part, in a world where the values of truth, personal honesty and a basic sense of what is right and wrong have been for so long flouted or only hypocritically retained that the only possible response is to withdraw to the marginalised role of independent moral arbitrator.

The very ease with which such apparently contrasting sociological 'equivalents' for Marlowe could be offered indicates that analysis along such lines would be lop-sided or wrong-headed; though it perhaps also suggests that the manifest differences between the proto-fascist, the reformist, and the decent moral conservative are differences only within a fundamentally shared perspective. However, to understand why the figure of Marlowe might be metamorphosed into such ostensibly diverse forms might be to uncover a potentially important permutation in the logic of norms and normality.

vi

What would it mean to 'understand' the figure of Marlowe? The type of analysis gestured at above approaches the text as a pattern of interrelated positions—those of Marlowe, the racketeers, the clients, the police— structurally homologous to some positions occupied or postulated in the 'actual' shape of a society, specifically a late capitalist society. But 'Marlowe' is, from another angle, only a name for the narrative strategy of the text.

At one level, 'Marlowe' is the narrating 'I', the offered and endorsed viewpoint of the text upon its proceedings; at another, 'Marlowe' is the *raison d'être* of the text: the plot, the characters, the action of the text serve to create and define the 'character' of 'Marlowe' as the unifying 'theme' of the whole reading experience of a Chandler novel. Our understanding of, and judgement upon, 'Marlowe' is the central component in our understanding of, and judgement upon, the novel as a whole; but equally our response to the novel is almost wholly shaped by our response to 'Marlowe'.

Obviously Chandler's novel is no different in this respect from many other novels narrated by their central protagonists. But since the 'content' of *The Big Sleep* is made up almost entirely of matters of 'law and order', of crime, corruption and violence, our response to those matters is also almost wholly shaped, in the reading experience, by our response to 'Marlowe'. But on what is that response based?

Primarily, it is based upon 'aesthetic' considerations—which need only at this point be indicated by differentiating them from 'moral' or 'rational' considerations: whereas in reading Poe or Conan Doyle we are mainly drawn into the process of 'ratiocination', and whereas in really encountering violence, corruption or crime we might be preoccupied by the 'moral' questions they pose for us, in reading Chandler we are primarily invited to appreciate the craft of the language, the skill of the construction, the orchestration of the action, the 'resolution' effected by the final chord. We are to enjoy the whole experience. Though the novels regularly 'deal with' such matters as criminal or police brutality, and the corruptions of the powerful or the 'law-abiding', these are proposed for our relaxed pleasure not our urgent response. The overall effect a Chandler novel aims for, and often achieves, is for the reader to close it with a sense of aesthetic satisfaction, of closure and finality, to recognise that this indeed is 'where it ends'—till the next novel.

I want to emphasise the obvious, but difficult, point that there is something deeply problematic about this textual strategy (though it is a totally familiar one, Chandler being merely a major exemplar in a long tradition). What is problematic is not that we should respond to such a novel according to primarily 'aesthetic' considerations, but rather that—once the fairly short-lived experiment in purely 'ratiocinative' detective fiction had lapsed—a reliance on familiar aesthetic criteria seemed the only possible alternative.

It is at this point that the real difficulty arises: for is there not a parallel in these terms to the shifts that Habermas's analysis of late capitalism indicates: that once the short-lived liberal-capitalist 'equilibrium', with its 'self-justifying' synthesis of economics, politics and morality (normality) had passed, any re-assertion of a 'rational' or even 'moral' basis for a system of law seemed untenable, and what did indeed take its place, for a time, in much of Europe, was an appeal to 'norms' which can in one sense be termed 'aesthetic', those norms embodied not in a formulated code but rather in a living focus and exemplar, *ein Führer*.

There is a crucial insight into Fascism in Walter Benjamin's remark: 'The logical result of Fascism is the introduction of aesthetics into political life'. His own analysis, limited to certain elements in Fascism, can help us to probe further. In 1936, in *The Work of Art in the Age of Mechanical Reproduction*, he argued:

> Fascism attempts to organise the newly created proletarian masses without affecting the property structure which the masses strive to eliminate. Fascism sees its salvation in giving these masses not their right, but instead a chance to express themselves. The masses have a right to change property relations; Fascism seeks to give them an expression while preserving property. The logical result of Fascism is the introduction of aesthetics into political life . . .
>
> All efforts to render politics aesthetic culminate in one thing: war. War and war only can set a goal for mass movements on the largest scale while respecting the traditional property system. This is the political formula for the situation. The technological formula may be stated as follows: Only war makes it possible to mobilize all of today's technical resources while maintaining the property system. It goes without saying that the Fascist apotheosis of war does not employ such arguments.

Among the 'arguments' that Fascism did employ was an appeal to nationalist fervour, but the concept of 'nation' has been, since at least the time of Herder, an aesthetic one. What 'defines' a 'nation' is a shared 'culture' rather than a geographical boundary, and what is meant by a 'culture' is inherently indefinable: the German or English 'way of life' is known only from the inside, by an intimacy of experience that cannot be fully articulated. What it means 'to be English' cannot be formulated with any precision; yet such phrases appeal to a sense of agreement: 'we know' what it is to be 'English'—if 'we' are 'English'. But of course the difficulty is that we thereby presume a 'norm' which we cannot even articulate in order to justify it; we may never be able to say with full conviction what constitutes a 'normal' English-man, but we harbour the deep delusion that, damn it all, some things just aren't normal for any normal English person—faced with the infinitely diverse activities, tastes, habits and life-experiences of fifty million people, a leap is made to the overarching hypothesis of some peculiarly 'English' characteristic which they share, and which rules them out of consideration if they don't. There is an even deeper delusion, often, that being 'English' is the normal thing for everyone to be—even Germans.

It is this fundamentally 'aesthetic' notion—neither rational nor moral nor immediately political—that not only underpins the appeal to militaristic nationalism (that patriotism which both justifies and makes possible war between 'nations', reshaping millions of different people into demarcated but homogenised national armies) but also fuels a deeply entrenched mode of reaction to developments within 'nations'. By an appeal to 'our English way of life' everything from changes in spelling practices to new fashions in dress, hairstyle or behaviour, from emerging forms of political agitation or economic struggle to ancient ways of making love, can be castigated and rejected as peculiarly 'offensive'—even when not (by some oversight) actually illegal or (was God nodding?) clearly immoral. The most dangerous manifestation of this irrational reaction is, of course, racism, not only in its more overtly and crassly 'cultural' forms (an outraged horror at an unfamiliar musical convention) but in its most genocidal: one reason for the extermination of six million Jews was that their very existence radically challenged the equation of 'culture' and 'nation' while at the same time embodying an intensive version of that equation.

The unwelcome ramifications of this 'aestheticisation of politics' have been apparent in many of the more intolerant and fearful twitchings of the traditional middle-class backlash in England, from the arrogant antics of Mary Whitehouse to the synthetic posturings of Margaret Thatcher. But the campaign to create in Thatcher the quintessentially 'British' woman was no accident: as in Nazi Germany, the logic of an appeal to an inexpressible 'nation' can only culminate in a politics of personality, in an 'image' in flesh of the living norm for a whole society. And, as in Nazi Germany, control over the mass media, the mass reproduction of images, is inevitably an important weapon in the aestheticisation of politics: it is in the daily dramatisation of a dramatised society that aestheticised politics finds its most pervasive expression.

Walter Benjamin, at the beginning of his 1936 essay, quotes a prophetic comment of Valery: 'Just as water, gas and electricity are brought into our houses from far off to satisfy our needs in response to a minimal effort, so we shall be supplied with visual or auditory images, which will appear and disappear at a simple movement of the hand, hardly more than a sign'. Benjamin's own concluding sentences in that essay are even more prophetic:

> '*Fiat ars—pereat mundus*', says Fascism, and, as Marinetti admits, expects war to supply the artistic gratification of a sense perception that has been changed by technology. This is evidently the consummation of *l'art pour l'art.* Mankind, which in Homer's time was an object of contemplation for the Olympian gods, now is one for itself. Its self-alienation has reached such a degree that it can experience its own destruction as an aesthetic pleasure of the first order. This is the situation of politics which Fascism is rendering aesthetic. Communism responds by politicising art.

In that final comment the work of, above all, Bertolt Brecht is broached: it was perhaps Brecht who found the most challenging way of developing beyond the ratiocinative element in art that had emerged so single-mindedly in Poe, without collapsing back into a safely 'aesthetic' response to crime, violence and corruption. Brecht's own direction had already been signalled in the title of his 1927 essay *Shouldn't we abolish Aesthetics?*

The logic of the aestheticisation of politics leads not only to a politics of personality but to a legislation of personalities. As the ineffable norm of national normality becomes the linchpin of a pervasive ideology, the pressure grows to extend the legal net to cover (once again?) more and more facets of life-style. If explicit criminalisation is not achieved, the grounds for suspicion of criminal intent are gradually extended to cover more and more 'questionable', 'undesirable', 'unconventional' modes of life and thought. That, in England now, someone is young, black and unemployed can be sufficient grounds to justify a body-search or arrest 'on suspicion'. That, in Germany now, someone once lived in the same house as a member of the KPD (Communist Party) can be sufficient grounds for depriving them of a teaching post. That, in the old Soviet Union now, someone has given an interview to an American journalist could be sufficient grounds for suspecting their sanity.

At the same rime, the aestheticisation of politics can increasingly diminish the possibility of any publicly canvassed alternative mode of political analysis. When 'scientific' psephology is the media's substitute for investigation of political demands, and the melodrama of personality-clashes in the House of Commons or the Cabinet replaces any coherent presentation and explanation of policies, the likelihood of even any feeble continuation of a 'system of parliamentary democracy' must be called in question. But in any case, one of the functions of the 'quasi-political compromise' of 'parliamentary democracy' is to obscure the basic structural contradiction of combining late capitalism with a non-totalitarian political system.

According to Raymond Chandler, 'All of my novels started from some known or unknown fact. Most of my work came from knowing or hearing of an inside news story that could not be published. Then fiction took over.' It was presumably not only Marlowe who, in *The Big Sleep*, was protecting the rich from the disclosure of their crimes.

It was once the ambition of fiction, and the hope of aesthetics, that in art the truth might be made public and apparent. As 'fiction' takes over in the late twentieth century its function may be, increasingly, to leave the truth concealed. Perhaps in that context it may be the critic who takes on the peculiarly ambivalent role of a private eye.

*

Q. 9: FRANZ KAFKA, *Der Prozess*

Kafka's *The Trial* begins: 'Someone must have been telling lies about Joseph K., for without having done anything wrong he was arrested one fine morning'.[6] Necessarily, Kafka is himself telling a kind of 'lie', since here he is asserting as 'true' something he knows not to be true: fiction is not truth—though neither is it untruth. But it is not necessarily Kafka who tells us that 'Someone must have been telling lies' and that K. was arrested 'without having done anything wrong', since the whole novel is written in a curious third-person subjective, from the viewpoint of the third-person singular that is 'he': the reader is formally restricted, by this textual strategy, to K.'s perspective throughout. Which means that K. may possibly be the 'someone' 'telling lies', since the question seemingly at issue is whether K. has done something 'wrong' or not. But even if we knew, from outside K.'s perspective, that K. had indeed committed some 'crime' we could not therefore conclude that K. was 'lying' in telling us (if he does) that he had done nothing wrong, since there is one difference between 'wrong' and 'crime' and another between 'telling a lie' and telling an 'untruth'. Fiction is a kind of 'lie' because we tell it 'as true' knowing it to be untrue; but we may even tell an untruth without lying provided we believe it to be true, just as we can lie while telling the truth provided we believe it (erroneously) to be untrue. We therefore have a logical criterion of lying even if we have no logical criterion of truth; but we have no empirical criterion of someone else lying (since the liar may be lying in telling us that he was or wasn't lying, and only he can tell us), even if we claim to have an empirical criterion of truth.

On the entangled but familiar logic of these problems the novel is constituted; on the logic of the same problems every legal trial which depends upon the distinction between

---

[6] Franz Kafka, *The Trial*, translated by Willa and Edwin Muir, Penguin edition, 1966, p.7; cited hereafter by page number only.

perjury and 'telling the truth' is vulnerable: when the accused pleads that he is 'not guilty' we, as jury, do not immediately believe him (otherwise there would be no trial); when a witness states his testimony we presume to believe it (otherwise there would be no witnessing). The relation between 'truth' and the various participants in a trial is curiously and interestingly diverse, yet for a trial to operate at all we must accept the risks of systematic and collusive lying among witnesses while discounting the plea of the accused as simply a necessary gesture in a ritual. (Perhaps only a 'show trial' which rests on an alternative notion of 'objective guilt' may escape these dilemmas.)

Throughout this novel, however, because of its third-person subjective viewpoint, we seem, as reader, to be allowed privileged access to precisely that area closed off to a law court: the mind of the accused. Surely we can therefore judge whether K. is lying or not, even if we cannot judge whether he is telling the truth. But because K. is never told of what he is accused, our privileged position does not allow us, or K. (unless he is lying), to know what it is that would crucially condemn him (at least as a perjurer) if he did lie. What we do know is that K. asserts that he wants to be acquitted and to be declared innocent. But there is another distinction between being acquitted and being innocent: given the problems (among others) of lying and perjury, it is possible both for the innocent to be found legally guilty and for the legally guilty to be in fact acquitted. Logically, indeed, only the accused could really judge his own innocence or guilt—of perjury at least. It is not necessary to his guilt or innocence that he be tried and found either legally guilty or legally not guilty. To believe that it is so necessary is to believe an untruth; to believe that it is not necessary and to assert that it is, even to oneself, is to lie.

Surely, a legal system, one might insist, cannot be concerned with guilt and innocence, only with the legal declaration of guilty or not-guilty; but then, of course, a legal trial cannot establish for the accused his guilt or innocence; any accused who thinks that it can is misled, and one who knows that it can't and yet insists that it can is lying. And yet what are guilt and innocence if they are not to be equated with legal guilt and non-guilt ? But if they are so equated a court has nothing to discover; it has only to pronounce. And if they are not so equated, what is it that a court finally pronounces upon? It seems necessary to assert that legal guilt is and is not to be equated with that guilt which is not merely legal guilt—but then no judgement can resolve its own ambivalent relation to the judgement it pronounces.

Kafka's novel twists some of these threads tighter at a moment when K. tells us, and himself, that he is lying. When the Priest finishes his last interpretation of the Parable of the Law, the text reads:

> 'I don't agree with that point of view,' said K., shaking his head, 'for if one accepts it, one must accept as true everything the doorkeeper says. But you yourself have sufficiently proved how impossible it is to do that.' 'No,' said the priest, 'it is not necessary to accept everything as true, one must only accept it as necessary.' 'A melancholy conclusion,' said K. 'It turns lying into a universal principle.' (p.243)

The exchange is a characteristic spiral of logic. K. concludes that if everything is to be accepted as necessary but not necessarily as true, then something may be necessary without being true, indeed everything may be necessary without being true: 'the lie' may indeed be 'the order of the world'[7] even if we cannot know whether it is—though if it might be, we would have to proceed on the assumption that nothing is true. (Such a world would be, perhaps, an anti-world to one of Hegel's.)

---

[7] To adapt the translation of this same phrase by Douglas Scott and Chris Waller in their translation of *The Trial*, Picador, 1977, p. 246.

Yet K.'s own conclusion depends, of course, upon a self-contradictory premise: if the priest's words are taken to apply to the world, rather than to the text of the parable, then they defeat themselves: if everything is to be accepted as necessary, it must also be necessary to accept everything as true—and as not true.

Alternatively, if it is not necessary to accept everything as true, we do not have to accept as true the claim that everything is necessary. And then to assert that something, or anything, is necessary may be to lie, not just to tell an untruth.

In any case, in saying that 'it turns lying into a universal principle' K. is already equivocating: 'K. said that with finality, but it was not his final judgement' (p.243). And immediately after, we are given an instance of him lying that something is necessary: the priest asks K. 'Do you want to leave already?', and 'although at that moment K. had not been thinking of leaving' he answers 'Of course, I must go'—yet a moment later we read: 'his immediate return to the Bank was not so necessary as he had made out, he could quite well stay longer'. Meanwhile, ' "You have to leave now," said the priest. "Well, yes," said K., "you must see that I can't help it." "You must first see that I can't help being what I am," said the priest' (p.244). K., we know (we think), is lying. The priest, we may suggest, is telling an untruth: 'I can't help being what I am.' If that were true, K. too, presumably, could not 'help' being what he is—in which case either he cannot be 'guilty' or his guilt is 'objective', determined in advance by what he cannot help (Astyanax in *The Trojan Women* comes to mind, not to speak of Calvin).

If we have to accept everything, including our own guilt or innocence, as unavoidable, as necessary, then we can make no sense of 'guilt' and 'innocence'. On the other hand, if we can 'help' being what we are, then what we are is not necessary, including what we are or do at any particular moment: to claim that we have to do anything, even to return to a Bank on time, would then be untrue; we do not even have to be at all, since our very existence or continued existence is not necessary. Indeed, the possibility that hovers over or underpins this logic is that nothing is necessary at all.

Though perhaps there is one exception: it may not be necessary that we be born, but once we are born it is indeed necessary that we die. The penultimate untruth—or desperate lie—that K. tells concerns the ancient, fatal syllogism: 'Logic is doubtless unshakable, but it cannot withstand a man who wants to go on living' (p.250). It can. It does. And as he dies K. utters the final self-deception: ' "Like a dog!" he said.' But he doesn't, and cannot, die 'like a dog', since, as Erich Fried—pursuing this logic—has written:[8]

> A dog that dies
> and that knows
> that it dies like a dog
> and that can say
> that it knows
> that it dies like a dog
> is a man.

One of the reasons why K. does not die like a dog is that (according to Wittgenstein at least)[9] 'a dog cannot be a hypocrite, but neither can it be sincere', and in judging his own dying to be like a dog's K. is perhaps sincere but, more likely, a hypocrite; he cannot be neither.

It would be possible both to pursue further the relations between truth, lying and necessity in *The Trial* itself and to examine related strands in Kafka's other work—for example in *The Judgement*, or *In the Penal Colony*, or, especially perhaps, in *The Castle*, where K.'s claim (lie?) that he is the Land

---

[8] Erich Fried, *On Pain of Seeing*, London 1969, p.11

[9] *Philosophical Investigations*, p. 229

Surveyor is the first of many exaggerations and deceptions which structure the life of the village and of the novel, and which are doubled in the exaggerated significance attached to the 'castle' by critics.

One could also analyse Kafka's own desperate attempts to be 'honest' about his own relationships in his correspondence with Milena and with Felice, or in his *Letter* to his father. His whole relationship with his father, and the connections between fatherhood and the 'law', could also be examined. Kafka's legal education, apprenticeship and work is obviously relevant (think of the attempted precision of his reports for the insurance company); so is his grasp of the 'religious' problem of 'The Fall' (think, for example, of the typical remark: 'Original sin, that old injustice committed by man, consists in the complaint unceasingly made by man that he has been the victim of an injustice, the victim of original sin'). It would also be feasible to sketch an analysis of *The Trial* in terms of the different ideological apparatuses focussed upon in each chapter, the whole under the dominion of 'the Law'. But though these facets are important, the central strategy of *The Trial* is to place the reader, alongside K., at the point where the 'logic, rules and procedures' of 'the law' converge: the position of the accused.

The 'accused' is a *necessary premise* for those rules and procedures, for that logic, to operate at all; but it is not necessary for the accused to be anyone in particular—the trial can, and will, proceed even if the accused is 'the wrong man'; it is not even legally necessary for the accused to be present at the trial, or even known (one can be accused 'with persons unknown'): a mere 'K.' or even a number can suffice on occasion. And perhaps, so long as there is, somewhere, an accused, there needn't, after all, be any specific accusation; certainly ,the 'wrong' accusation is no impediment to the logic of the court: the rules of logic are not contingent upon any specific content.

As we read *The Trial* we ourselves supply, perhaps necessarily, a content for that unformulated accusation: we too are caught within the process of the text, we too begin to 'tell lies' about 'K.', perhaps to accuse him (in our 'interpretations') of crimes, or wrongs, or faults, which we guiltily feel ourselves to be accused of by the novel, or which we (innocently, and erroneously) think are somehow 'necessary' crimes. At that point we should perhaps recognise that we have placed ourselves in the dock with K.: prosecutor and accused change places, or perhaps their functions fuse—as in the initial plea of some accused: 'Guilty'. It is the logic of that situating which we can see being worked through in novels subsequent to Kafka.

(Unfinished—no time)

*

Q. 12 : ALBERT CAMUS, *La Chute*

> For if the Idea of Beauty appears only in dispersed form among many works, each one nevertheless aims uncompromisingly to express the whole of beauty, claims it in its singularity and can never admit its dispersal without annulling itself. Beauty, as single, true and liberated from appearance and individuation, manifests itself not in the synthesis of all works, in the unity of the arts and of art, but only as a physical reality: in the downfall of art itself. This downfall is the goal of every work of art, in that it seeks to bring death to all others. That all art aims to end art, is another way of saying the same thing. It is this impulse to self-destruction inherent in works of art . . that is constantly stirring up the aesthetic disputes that are apparently so futile.
>
> Theodor Adorno, *Minima Moralia*

Fully to situate Camus's *The Fall* (1956) would involve considering, at least, his pre-war membership of the Algerian Communist Party, his passion for truthful reporting while working for *Alger Republicain*, his treatment of the relationship between a moment of 'crime' and the procedures of the law-court in *L'Étranger* (1940), his involvement with the Resistance and, particularly, his dispute with Mauriac over the capital punishment of French traitors after the war, his quarrel with Sartre over Sartre's reaction to *L'Homme Revolté* (1951)—during which Sartre described Camus's position as that of a paternalistic 'advocate' for the oppressed, the impact of Kafka's work on Camus's 'philosophy', the general impact of Koestler's *Darkness at Noon* (published in France in 1946) on the French debate about the Soviet concentration camps (see Merleau-Ponty's *Humanism and Terror* for something of that debate) and —perhaps most centrally—Camus's political silence on the Algerian situation from 1945 to 1954 and his opposition to the FLN thereafter[10]. But it is on the strategies and tactics of the text itself that I want to focus.

One immediate indication of the basic strategy of the text is retained in French even in the English translation[11]: the shifting terms of address used by Clamence to his listener — *Monsieur* (p. 5ff), *Monsieur et cher compatriote* (p. 13ff), *cher Monsieur* (p. 16ff), *mon cher compatriote* (p. 33ff), *cher ami* (p. 54ff), *mon cher ami* (p. 57ff), *mon cher* (p. 72), *cher ami* (p. 78), *mon ami* (p. 87), *très cher* (p. 100) and, finally, *cher maître* in the closing words of the book.

That gradual increase in familiarity is an index to the relationship that is courteously and skilfully established and confirmed and it is one not only between Clamence and his silent listener but also between Clamence and the reader, who, in 'silently' reading the monologue of *The Fall*, enacts the voice of Clamence, plays the role of the speaker to whom the reader also 'silently' listens. The reader is positioned as both of the actors in this dramatic monologue that is a 'dialogue of a special kind'.

From the opening of the text the reader is offered a double-role which he (and perhaps she?) remains as free to refuse as a bar-room customer approached by a stranger: 'May I, Monsieur, offer my services without running the risk of intruding?' (p. 5). To accept such an offer is always a risk; to go on reading is always a risk. Mockingly, the reader, in the guise of that silent drinker in an Amsterdam bar, is given his opportunity for refusal: 'Now I shall withdraw, Monsieur, happy to have been of help to you. Thank you; I'd accept if I were sure of not being a nuisance. You are too kind. Then I shall bring my glass over beside yours' (p. 5).

From that moment it will take more than discourtesy or rudeness to slide away; it will soon take a kind of cowardice. Within a page our own reactions are being both responded to and prompted by the text: 'If that be foolish . . Ah, I see

---

10 See, for example, Conor Cruise O'Brien, *Camus*, London 1970, pp. 64-75.

11 See A. Camus, *The Fall*, translated by Justin O'Brien, Penguin edition, 1963, cited hereafter by page number only.

you smile at that use of the subjunctive' (p. 6); and soon we are offered a description which we, perhaps, uneasily, admit does, more or less, in a way, fit us:

> Pleased to know you. You are in business, no doubt? In a way? Excellent reply! Judicious too: in all things we are merely 'in a way'. Now, allow me to play the detective. You are my age in a way, with the sophisticated eye of the man in his forties who has seen everything, in a way; you are well dressed in a way, that is as people are in our country; and your hands are smooth. Hence a bourgeois, in a way! But a cultured bourgeois! Smiling at the use of the subjunctive, in fact, proves your culture twice over because you recognise it to begin with and then because you feel superior to it. Lastly, I amuse you. And be it said without vanity, this implies in you a certain open-mindedness. Consequently you are in a way. . But no matter. Professions interest me less than sects. Allow me to ask you two questions and don't answer if you consider them indiscreet. Do you have any possessions? Some? Good. Have you shared them with the poor? No? Then you are what I call a Sadducee. If you are not familiar with the Scriptures, I admit that this won't help you. But it does help you? So you know the Scriptures? Decidedly, you interest me. (pp. 8-9)

By this stage we know that our interlocutor calls himself a 'judge-penitent' (p. 8), which may merely suggest a penitent judge, or perhaps a modern version of a friar-penitent, but hints in either case at a curious fusion of roles normally separated: someone positioned simultaneously as judge (about to judge) and as penitent (the accused already found guilty and undergoing penance). We have been steered away from judging in the first few pages ('Mind you, I'm not judging him', p. 6; 'Still, let us take care not to condemn him', p. 7), but now we are explicitly invited to judge the judge-penitent himself: 'As for me . . Well, judge for yourself.' (p. 9).

At the second meeting (perhaps with that mockingly polite invitation still in our ears—'Try it!', p. 14), we are given more upon which to judge, as Clamence unfolds the story of his life in Paris, a life that he can summarise at this stage in ostensibly self-satisfied phrases:

> . . just imagine, I beg you, a man at the height of his powers, in perfect health, generously gifted, skilled in bodily exercises as in those of the mind, neither rich nor poor, sleeping well and fundamentally pleased with himself without showing this otherwise than by a happy sociability. You will readily see how I can speak, without immodesty, of a successful life. (p. 22)

No reader can, I presume, get this far without a certain unease or even revulsion at Clamence's self-description: the whole portrait has a subtle tone of corruption about it, an ideal turned into a perversity. Like J. H. Newman's description of the liberal English gentleman, this portrait seems pervasively yet never precisely askew to the model it simultaneously evokes yet undermines. The question that is being put to us already is: 'by what standards are you judging?'

For in the complex interplay of this whole passage (pp. 15-32) a number of possible grounds for an adverse judgement are both suggested and allowed for in advance. If we sense that Clamence is selfish, he counters with an implicit appeal to an Aristotelian definition—'I enjoyed my own nature to the fullest and we all know that therein lies happiness, although, to soothe one another mutually, we occasionally pretend to condemn such joys as selfishness'—and we are forced to ponder that 'pretend'.

If we lean towards pride or hypocrisy as Clamence's crucial fault, we have to recognise that the hypocrisy and pride are accompanied by a peculiar honesty and humility, since it is Clamence himself who paints this double-faced portrait. In any case, which Clamence are we judging?

If we feel that the Clamence of his 'Edenic' period (cf. p. 22) is to be judged severely, or even adversely, is it not the Clamence now speaking who allows us to see that—and doesn't that rather qualify our judgement?

The tactic of this section is perhaps signalled in those two separated but mutually-echoing comments: 'we have to have judges, don't we?' (p. 16) and 'it set me above the judge whom I judged in turn' (p. 11). We feel called upon to judge this self-portrait while sensing that the man who provides it has already, like a subtle Titorelli, foreseen and reckoned with our judgement.

And if we settle back to follow this complex game with mere accepting amusement, we are ambushed in our smile by the comment: 'My reflection was smiling in the mirror, but it seemed to me that my smile was double . . ' (p. 31). This sense of the complex joke being against us is uneasily confirmed by the last few sentences of this section:

> If pimps and thieves were invariably sentenced, all decent people would get to thinking they themselves were constantly innocent, *cher Monsieur*. And in my opinion—all right, all right, I'm coming!—that's what must be avoided at all costs. Otherwise, everything would be just a joke. (p. 32)

As the monologue of the third meeting develops, the tactic of the text becomes even clearer: the examples of behaviour we feel called upon to disapprove of multiply and begin to rouse uneasy echoes of our own behaviour; each reader is being prompted to a self-recognition in at least some of the incidents and attitudes that are laid before us — and each will respond to a different pattern in this skilfully constructed account. No reader will have experienced quite the same rankling humiliations or utilised exactly the same devious stratagems as Clamence, but the details of the text serve by this stage very much as cues to our own memories, trailers for those 'little films' we too run 'a hundred times' in our imagination—or which we slyly censor even in our private cinema. The invitation is by now explicit:

> . . if everyone told all, displayed his true profession and identity, we shouldn't know which way to turn! Just fancy visiting cards: Dupont, jittery philosopher, or Christian landowner, or adulterous humanist—indeed,

> there's a wide choice. But it would be hell! Yes, hell must be like that: streets filled with shop-signs and no way of explaining oneself. One is classified once and for all.
>
> You, for instance, *mon cher compatriote*, stop and think of what your sign would be. You are silent? Well, you'll tell me later on. (p. 36)

When, finally, we are given the incident at the 'centre' of Clamence's memory—the girl on the bridge, the fall, the hesitation, the turning away—its details are specific (so specific as to leave judgement, like decision, finely poised in welcome doubt), but its significance is general; we could all disclaim any definite action, any particular commission; it is harder to maintain our innocence when accused, however implicitly, of inaction, of hesitation, of turning away, of the sin of *omission.*

The next two sections can be slid over quickly here—since they offer themselves, to some extent, precisely as temptations to that response: 'the question is how to slip through and, above all—yes, above all, the question is how to elude judgement' (p. 57). But the final section repeats and makes explicit the strategy of the whole:

> I know what you're thinking: it's very hard to disentangle the true from the false in what I'm saying. I admit you're right. I myself— (p. 88)

That broken, suspended phrase allows us to register, quite clearly, the Camus who offers himself as, in part, Clamence. One of the temptations of the text is to read it as autobiographical, as confessional, in however displaced a fashion, for Camus himself. It is a comforting way of distancing Clamence from ourselves. The paragraph continues on a different tack:

> You see, a person I knew used to divide human beings into three categories: those who prefer having nothing to hide rather than being obliged to lie, those who prefer lying to having nothing to hide, and finally those

> who like both lying and the hidden. I'll let you choose which case suits me best. (p. 88)

The reader has also, by this stage, to choose which category suits the reader best—or if he rejects the categories offered, to decide what he would say instead. For it is clear that the grip of the text has been all along designed to close upon the reader:

> . . in short I adapt my words to my listener and lead him to go me one better. I mingle what concerns me and what concerns others, I choose the features we have in common, the experiences we have endured together, the failings we share—good form, the man of the moment, in fact, such as reigns in me and in others. With all that I construct a portrait which is the image of all and of no one. A mask, in short, rather like those carnival masks which are both lifelike and stylised so that they make people say: 'Why, surely I've met him!' When the portrait is finished, as it is this evening, I show it with great sorrow: 'This, alas, is what I am!' The prosecutor's charge is finished. But at the same time the portrait I hold out to my contemporaries becomes a mirror. (p. 102)

By this mirror-portrait:

> I provoke you into judging yourself, and this relieves me of that much of the burden. Ah, *mon cher*, we are odd, wretched creatures and, if we merely look back over our lives, there's no lack of occasions to amaze and scandalise ourselves. Just try. I shall listen, you may be sure, to your own confession with a great feeling of fraternity. (p. 103)

Of course, Clamence cannot listen to *our* confession. The whole operation of the text, as text, is necessarily one-sided. But to read the text is to enter into a complex dialectic, a dialogical relation with ourselves, the end-term of which may well be a curious kind of confession.

At the centre of that dialectic is Clamence's 'judgement' on Clamence, not only the Clamence of his Edenic days but the Clamence who speaks in the present: 'I haven't changed my way of life; I continue to love myself and to make use of others' (p. 104). But we also, as reader, are provoked to judge Clamence's judgement of himself, and insofar as we recognise the distance between Clamence and Camus we are faced with the task of understanding Camus's judgement on his own character Clamence (and perhaps also the judgement on an earlier, or present, Camus expressed through that character). But we have also, then, to judge those judgements of Camus—while at the same time Camus is, by the very complexity of his text, testing our own capacity for judgement: at what points, and for what reasons, do we stand back from Clamence and refuse his attitudes, opinions, judgements? The crucial question is: for what reasons? If we can articulate the grounds of our 'judgement' in this multi-layered (perhaps indeed: multi-lawyered) case, what are they? One might even ask what kind of 'grounds' are they? Or do we have any at all?

One easy, distancing, response is to treat the novel firmly as a disguised polemic, with pre-chosen and safely remote targets: as, for example, 'a satirical portrait of left-wing intellectuals as Camus saw them, lost in the nihilistic desert of 20th century ideologies, led astray by their own systematic abstractions' (to quote Emmett Parker). The epigraph from Lermontov lends some support to this kind of reading:

> Some were dreadfully insulted, and quite seriously, to have held up as a model such an immoral character as *A Hero of Our Time*; others shrewdly noticed that the author had portrayed himself and his acquaintances . . *A Hero of Our Time*, gentlemen, is in fact a portrait but not of an individual; it is the aggregate of the vices of our whole generation in their fullest expression.

But that 'shrewdly' may rather register an ironic anticipation of a predictable interpretation, while that final sentence merely brings us back to the problem of judging the 'vices' we are invited to recognise—and of judging them to be vices in the first place.

If we duck the problem of 'judging' then we are perhaps reproducing the 'fall' that is at the centre of the novel: we take note of the problem, recognise it as a difficult and demanding problem, and then turn away. The logic of that refusal is either to decline the intrusion of Clamence in the first place (never really to read the text) or to close the novel merely with the relief of having it behind us, a safe and distanced memory of reading ('Fortunately'). On the basis of either response we can, coolly, skilfully, professionally, 'place' the novel in its 'historical' context, as time passed, as past time.

Another, familiar, response is to opt, respectfully, perhaps 'critically', for an 'aesthetic' judgement upon *The Fall* 'as a novel'—to quote, for example, Sartre's moving and eloquent tribute:

> One lived with or against his thought, such as he revealed it to us in his books—*La Chute*, above all, perhaps the most beautiful and the least understood—but always through it. It was a singular adventure of our culture, a movement whose phases and final term one tried to guess.

—and to pick out that phrase, 'the most beautiful and the least understood', and, after some suitable elaboration, to leave it, more or less, at that. Such an 'aesthetic' or 'literary critical' response must seem inadequate; but perhaps it holds a clue to the paradox and the pressure of the actual reading experience of the novel.

At one point in the text we are reminded of a certain kind of 'aesthetic judgement'. Clamence justifies his retention of the painting of *The Just Judges*, the stolen panel from the Van Eyck altarpiece *The Adoration of the Lamb*, and offers, among other reasons, the claim that: 'among all those who file past *The Adoration of the Lamb* no one could distinguish the copy from the original.' (p. 95)

To file past the copy in reverent admiration, accepting the pre-packaged judgement of the guide-book, is merely to consume a cultural commodity, to clock up an item in a tourist's self-improvement schedule. Of course, those who have the expensive privilege of not merely filing past but may linger to appreciate and analyse, might protest that they at least, the dedicated experts, can indeed 'distinguish the copy from the original': given the very materiality of the art-object in this case, a 'copy' could be easily detected by the useful, though of course ancillary, scientific tests of the auctioneer; and given the other 'authentic' panels of the polyptych any well-trained art-historian could heuristically sketch the missing components and assess a forgery against that absent ideal, even if the missing bit had never been known to them (though in this case, as Camus perhaps knew, the Van Eyck altarpiece is noticeably 'incoherent' by the received standards of the art-historians of the period).

But if our task is neither to nod with passing second-hand awe nor to carbon-date an expensive investment, what is our response to be? If we seek to make that kind of 'judgement' known as 'aesthetic', what is the basis for our judgement?

Walter Benjamin,[12] meditating on that ancient distinction between the 'original' and the 'copy' (Plato in his own way was concerned with it), probed the effects of dislodging the art-object from its cultic niche and function. He argues that the 'aura' of the original is dissolved in the era of technical reproduction, leaving behind only muffled and ambivalent traces in the practices of cultural exhibition (one aim of which is, arguably, to enhance the 'aura' of the original precisely as 'an original'). More crucially, when the processes of artistic production render the notion of *any* 'original' unintelligible (to ask for the 'authentic' print makes no sense—did it ever make sense to ask for the 'authentic' *Hamlet*?—for different reasons), then 'the total function of art is reversed: instead of being based on ritual, it begins to

---

[12] Walter Benjamin, *The Work of Art in the Age of Mechanical Reproduction.*

be based on politics'. But before we return to Benjamin's insight here, it is worth detouring through a phase he does not consider.

The 'novel' is already an example of a 'work of art in an age of mechanical reproduction': it never made any sense to ask for the 'original copy' (not the manuscript or the first edition) of *Tom Jones*. At the moment of appearance of *Tom Jones* one kind of response to it was already formed and waiting, a reaction exemplified in Samuel Johnson's comment, recounted by Hannah More:

> I never saw Johnson really angry with me but once, and his displeasure did him so much honour that I loved him the better for it. I alluded rather flippantly, I fear, to some witty passage in *Tom Jones*: he replied, 'I am shocked to hear you quote from so vicious a book. I am sorry to hear you have read it; a confession which no modest lady should ever make. I scarcely know a more corrupt work.'

Sir John Hawkins spelt out the basis of Johnson's reaction in a celebrated piece of invective against *Tom Jones*:

> . . a book seemingly intended to sap the foundation of that morality which it is the duty of parents and all public instructors to inculcate in the minds of young people, by teaching that virtue upon principle is imposture, that generous qualities alone constitute true worth, and that a young man may love and be loved, and at the same time associate with the loosest women. His morality, in that it resolves virtue into good affections, in contra-diction to moral obligation and a sense of duty, is that of Lord Shaftesbury vulgarised, and is a system of excellent use in palliating the vices most injurious to society. He was the inventor of that cant-phrase 'goodness of heart', which is every day used as a substitute for probity, and means little more than the virtue of a horse or a dog: in short, he has done more towards corrupting the rising generation than any writer we know of.

Hawkins and Johnson, in accusing Fielding of philosophical naivety about the nature of morality are also clearly condemning Fielding's novel. (Like Rubashov in *Darkness At Noon*, perhaps, they do not accept that 'subjective' intention or personal character can take precedence over the 'objective' principles by which we should be governed.)

That interpenetration of moral and 'critical' judgement is, of course, inherited, endorsed and perpetuated in an English critical tradition that passes through Matthew Arnold to F. R. Leavis—Leavis's refusal to give the ultimate 'grounds' of his criticism was due, in its way, to a sound eighteenth-century instinct, just as his sense of personal 'authority' has one of its roots in that eighteenth-century practice, instanced in a letter of Goldsmith's in 1758, of awarding poets marks out of twenty for 'Judgement' —the critic himself necessarily scoring the maximum.

T. S. Eliot indicated one undercurrent in this censorious tradition when he remarked: 'I view Johnson's *Lives* as a master-piece of the judicial bench'. Fielding himself had already recognised the parallel (it is more than a parallel for him):

> I must desire all those critics to mind their own business, and not to intermeddle with affairs or works which in no ways concern them; for till they produce the authority by which they are constituted judges, I shall not plead to their jurisdiction.
>
> (*Tom Jones*, I, ii)

> I shall not look upon myself as accountable to any court of critical jurisdiction whatever; for as I am, in reality, the founder of a new province of writing, so I am at liberty to make what laws I please therein.
>
> (*Tom Jones*, II, ii)

One effect of that tradition of interweaving 'aesthetic, 'moral' and 'judicial' criticism is perhaps to allow political judgements to appear in 'criticism' in a disarmingly disguised form—as in the judicial pronouncements of the Old Bailey, or the moral judgements of the BBC censors, or the aesthetic policy declarations of the Arts Council.

But another effect has been to help engender an apparently opposite reaction: the radical separation of the 'aesthetic' from any other kind of judgement, including 'moral' and 'political' (precisely the rationale of the Arts Council). In its more sophisticated form—popularly articulated by Oscar Wilde in the preface to *The Picture of Dorian Gray*—this latter reaction proposed *l'art pour l'art*; in its popular form—still sophisticatedly articulated by a host of smoothly privileged pundits—this reaction led to an enthroning of 'taste'.

Benjamin sketches another, and more basic, reason for this double-faceted counter-tradition:[13]

> Taste develops with the definite preponderance of commodity production over any other kind of production. As a consequence of the manufacture of products as commodities for the market, people become less and less aware of the conditions of their production—not only of the social conditions in the form of exploitation, but of the technical conditions as well. . . In the same measure as the expertness of a customer declines, the importance of his taste increases—both for him and for the manufacturer. For the customer it has the value of a more or less elaborate masking of his lack of expertness. . . It is precisely this development which literature reflects in *l'art pour l'art*. This doctrine and its corresponding practice for the first time give taste a dominant position in poetry. . . In *l'art pour l'art* the poet for the first time faces language the way the buyer faces the commodity on the open market. He has lost his familiarity with the process of its production to a particularly high degree. The poets of *l'art pour l'art* are the last about whom it can be said that they come 'from the people'. They have nothing to formulate with such urgency that it could determine the

[13] Walter Benjamin, *Charles Baudelaire*, London 1973, p.104.

> coining of their words. Rather, they have to choose their words. . . The poet of *l'art pour l'art* wanted to bring to language above all himself—with all the idiosyncracies, nuances, and imponderables of his nature. These elements are reflected in taste. The poet's taste guides him in his choice of words. . . At the end of this development may be found Mallarmé and the theory of *poésie pure*. There the cause of his own class has become so far removed from the poet that the problem of a literature without an object becomes the centre of discussion.

This passage is best understood not in terms of its 'juxtapositionism'—its yoking together of commercial developments 'and' literary developments—but rather as indicating a specific series of shifts 'within' the cultural apparatus; it echoes Bertolt Brecht's note on 'The Reading of Plays', concerning *Threepenny Opera*:

> Its publication represents little more than the prompt book of a play wholly surrendered to theatres, and thus is directed at the expert rather than at the consumer. This doesn't mean that the conversion of the maximum number of readers or spectators into experts is not thoroughly desirable; indeed it is under way.

Adorno suggests a perhaps more generous account of *l'art pour l'art* than Benjamin: that, to adapt E. P. Thompson's phrase about law, it was concerned with art's 'own logic, rules and procedures'—that is, with art simply as art. In his *Philosophy of Modem Music* Adorno offers an account which is partly complementary to Benjamin's (as concerned with changes in artist-audience relations) but which, in considering also a later phase, and a different art-form, partly disputes Benjamin's implicit evaluation and certainly refuses Brecht's optimism:[14]

---

[14] T. W. Adorno, *Philosophy of Modem Music*, London 1973, p.8.

> From the middle of the nineteenth century on, good music has renounced commercialism altogether. The consequence of its further development has come into conflict with the manipulated and, at the same time, self-satisfied needs of the bourgeois public. The pathetically small number of connoisseurs was gradually replaced by all those who could afford the price of a ticket and wished to demonstrate their culture to others. An abyss developed between public taste and compositional quality . . .Radically modem music could no longer count on . . support. Quality may be determined according to the same standards in advanced works as well as in traditional works—perhaps even more easily—despite the limitations of these standards. The prevailing musical language no longer removes the burden of accuracy and integrity from the shoulders of the composer. At the same time, the self-appointed mediators have sacrificed their capacity to make such judgements. Since the compositional procedure is gauged simply according to the inherent form of every work—not according to tacitly accepted, general demands—it is no longer possible to 'learn' definitively what constitutes good or bad music. Whoever would pass judgement must face squarely the immutable questions and antagonisms of the individual compositional structure, about which no general music history can teach. No one could be better suited to this task than the progressive composer, whom discursive reasoning most eludes. He can no longer depend upon mediators between himself and the public. Critics live literally according to the 'high reason' expressed in the song by Gustav Mahler: they evaluate according to what they do and do not understand.

These comments by Adorno bring us back to one phrase in Sartre's remark about *The Fall*: 'perhaps the most beautiful and the least understood'. For Adorno, a 'critic' will only venture to evaluate positively what he 'already' understands, but such a critic is debarred from that very 'familiarity with the process of . . production' which is the only basis for 'understanding' when the object of evaluation is 'the inherent form' of 'the individual compositional structure', its peculiar 'questions and antagonisms'.

It is, for Adorno, the 'radical' composer who (despite Benjamin's counter-case) is most 'expertly' concerned with the 'material' which is 'included in the process of . . . production' of art, whether that 'material' be musical or linguistic. But to speak of 'the inherent form' (as Adorno does) and of the 'material' (as I have just done) of a work of art is to reintroduce a distinction which Benjamin at least struggled to reject: that between 'form' and 'content', precisely the distinction which is at issue in the conflation of 'moral' and 'aesthetic' judgement and which haunts the long debate about 'politics' and 'art'.

At this point we can return again to *The Fall*. I suggested earlier that the problem posed for the reader by the strategy of the novel is that in reading the novel he is drawn into a complex dialectic of judging judgements and is thereby invited to reflect upon the grounds of his own judgement. Towards the end of the penultimate meeting Clamence speaks of himself as 'Elijah without a messiah', 'showering imprecations on lawless men who cannot endure any judgement', and he comments:

> He who clings to a law does not fear the judgement that puts him in his place within an order he believes in. But the keenest of human torments is to be judged without law. Yet we are in that torment. (p. 86)

The 'torment' that faces the critic who attempts to 'judge' a work, the 'inherent form' of which is closed to him, is that of 'judging without law', of attempting to come to a 'judgement' while being ignorant of the 'law' that governs the object of that judgement. (One could reformulate along these lines Fielding's remarks about critics and about making what 'laws' he pleases in his new province of writing.)

The same could be said of the composer himself, on Adorno's account: for if 'the prevailing musical language no longer removes the burden of accuracy and integrity from the shoulders of the composer' and if 'the compositional procedure is gauged simply according to the inherent form of every work' and if, finally, 'whoever would pass judgement must face squarely the immutable questions and antagonisms of the individual compositional structure', then how is the composer to 'judge' his 'own' composition and what would it mean for him to do so? In the actual process of production the composer would seem to face most acutely that 'torment' of judging (and of being judged) 'without law', without the already achieved 'inherent form' of the 'compositional structure' which provides its own 'logic, rules and procedures'.

There is, of course, a readily-available 'Romantic' version of that 'torment': the agonies of creation, the struggle with the inner soul seeking expression; and in that hybrid character Adrian Leverkuhn we can discern a daemonic variation of that torment. But there is always a more prosaic and certainly more practical question the artist has to answer: at what point is the work finished, when is the process of production over? And one way of approaching that question is to explore the problem of the 'unity' of the work of art (a problem that could be formulated in terms of a 'missing' panel from a polyptych).

Adorno remarks that 'no one could be better suited to this task [of 'judgement'] than the progressive composer, whom discursive reasoning most eludes'. Adorno's own favoured candidate as 'progressive composer' is Schoenberg, and a comment by Heinze-Klaus Metzger on Schoenberg's *First String Quartet, in D minor, opus 7*, may help us to grasp the kind of non-'discursive' 'reason' which informs it:[15]

> By using multiple counterpoint on a small fund of basic material Schoenberg achieves a wide variety of motives and thematic figures. No generally applied method is used; the dialectic between particular and general is always real, and is never allowed to relax into a harmonious balance. The result, so far as the overall

[15] Sleeve-note to recording *DGG* 2530 329

> form is concerned, was a work which is simultaneously in one movement and in four movements, one in which the usual four movements of large-scale cyclic sonata form are compressed into a single one, in such a way that their relationships to one another constitute a sonata form of a higher logical order. Thus for example the 'slow movement' takes on the function of a 'second subject' within the overall sonata, and the development technique which proliferates throughout the whole work . . . like the localized transition sections, is always logically polyvalent, having a function both in terms of each particular formal part of lower or higher significance, and within the larger sections or the overall form. This state of affairs, taken in conjunction with the inexhaustible contrapuntal combinations, some-times leads one to think of Freud's concept of over-determination, in which case the compositional economy of the work could also be interpreted as a criticism of this compositional economy; perhaps the most fruitful aspect of a dialectic whose task, according to Adorno, is to break through the constrictive nature of logic with the aid of logic's own means.

Registering the allusion to Freud, and the final comment about a 'dialectic' that seeks to 'break through the constrictive nature of logic with the aid of logic's own means', we might now recall Freud's own comments on the relation of the dream-work to 'logic':[16]

> We are here interested only in the essential dream-thoughts. These usually emerge as a complex of thoughts and memories of the most intricate possible structure, with all the attributes of the trains of thought familiar to us in waking life. They are not infrequently trains of thought starting out from more than one centre, though having points of contact. Each train of thought is almost invariably accompanied by its

[16] Sigmund Freud, *The Interpretation of Dreams*, ch. V.

contradictory counterpart, linked with it by antithetical association. The different portions of this complicated structure stand, of course, in the most manifold logical relations to one another. They can represent foreground and background, digressions and illustrations, conditions, chains of evidence and counter-arguments. When the whole mass of these dream-thoughts is brought under the pressure of the dream-work, and its elements are turned about, broken into fragments and jammed together—almost like pack-ice—the question arises of what happens to the logical connections which have hitherto formed its framework. What representation do dreams provide for 'if', 'because', 'just as', 'although', 'either-or', and all the other conjunctions without which we cannot understand sentences or speeches?

In the first resort our answer must be that dreams have no means at their disposal for representing these logical relations between the dream-thoughts. For the most part dreams disregard all these conjunctions, and it is only the substantive content of the dream-thoughts that they take over and manipulate. The restoration of the connections which the dream-work has destroyed is a task which has to be performed by the interpretative process.

For Freud, 'the incapacity of dreams to express these things must lie in the nature of the psychical material out of which dreams are made'. But in discussing the procedures, devices, rules by which the dream-work operates—displacement, con-densation and overdetermination—and in probing the 'psychical material' out of which they are 'made', Freud too seems to operate with a distinction between 'content' (both manifest and latent) and 'form'; for Freud the dream-work is the 'dream' yet he can also write[17] that the dream-work 'is under some kind of necessity to combine all the sources

[17] See *Standard Edition, IV*, p. 179.

which have acted as stimuli for the dream into a single unity'.

The problem here is not what is that 'necessity' that governs the operation of the dream-work, but rather how we are to conceive of that 'unity' demanded by that 'necessity'. Insofar as the 'dream-work' achieves its object, insofar as it makes sense to speak of 'a' dream, how are we to speak of the 'unity' of that dream?

Benjamin writes of the poets of *l'art pour l'art* as having 'nothing to formulate with such urgency that it could determine the coining of their words', their 'choice of words' being 'made only among words which have not already been coined by the object itself'. To coin a word is always to seek to escape the pull of existing words, to wrench and dislocate the language of our thought.

We need a word (a 'concept') which is neither 'form' nor 'content', which can allow us to speak of that 'unity' which is the object of the dream-work and its product, a word which may also enable us to speak of the art-work's achievement of 'unity'.

Freud speaks of the aim of the dream as 'wish-fulfilment'. We can take one overtone of that term, together with a pun on 'content', and speak of the '*contentment*' sought by the dream-work; and we can take the chiming word '*containment*', as indicating that the 'dream' 'contains' its 'content' not as a container but rather in the way a quarrel is 'contained', made tolerable, held in check, without being resolved or defused —anger or impatience which is 'contained' is only partially repressed. And, finally, we can take the overtones of 'pressure' in 'repressed', together with an undersense of 'select' or 'sieve', and speak of the '*strain*' which characterises the dream-work.

Fusing these terms, a verbal noun can be coined: '*constraint-ment* '—an action, process, work, whose gradually achieved effect is constraintment, the dream-work arrives at self-constraintment. Condensation and displacement are devices, tactics, which serve and are parts of the process which is self-constraintment. The dream-work's self-constraintment is always precarious, however, since the necessity for it, what makes it necessary, is finally insatiable, uncontainable, dis-contented, unconstrainable: the 'dream' is a moment of truce in an *agon* the only end of which is death and which started with birth itself.

If we think of the art-work also in these terms, or with this term, Adorno's phrase 'the immutable questions and antagonisms of the individual compositional structure', and Metzger's 'dialectic' which seeks 'to break through the constrictive nature of logic with the aid of logic's own means', can now lead us back to the 'logical' problem which confronts the reader of *The Fall*.

It would be possible to formulate that problem in familiar 'logical' terms: is it possible to make a ('legal') judgement 'without law'? That problem, in its manifold variations, could be tracked through the well-worn debates in the philosophy of law, or pursued into political or moral philosophy, or elaborated according to endless constitutional permutations on the 'separation of powers'. The logic of the ideology of law has its own interminability.

The task of the 'text' of *The Fall* is not, however, to 'answer' the 'immutable questions and antagonisms' that arise within that ideologic; it is to 'arrive at' their *self-constraintment*, to 'hold' the conflict of 'thoughts and memories of the most intricate possible' kind.

Those 'trains of thoughts and memories' which are self-constrainted as *The Fall* can be traced back through Camus's other writings, his life, his 'whole generation', the whole history of an epoch, just as the trains of thoughts and memories which traverse our different 'readings' of *The Fall* could also be traced till they are lost over numerous personal and epochal horizons: those trains start out 'from more than one centre, though having points of contact' and 'each train of thought is almost invariably accompanied by its contradictory counterpart, linked with it by antithetical association'.

A certain kind of 'criticism' seeks to trace those chains and trains, those thoughts and memories; such criticism is interminable.

There is another kind of 'criticism' which seeks to 'understand' the 'logic' that is at work in the process of self-constraintment, or which is itself in the process of self-constraintment. In doing so, such criticism may lay bare the ideological questions and antagonisms, contradictions and conundrums, which formed the 'frame-work' for the work of constraintment. The 'restoration of the connections' which set the art-work in motion may be 'a task which has to be performed by the interpretative process' of this kind of criticism.

But the actual writing of *The Fall*, the work of arriving at the final text, is not an exercise in 'discursive reasoning'. Rather, it consists in the difficult work of turning the 'logic' of an ideologic back upon itself, manipulating its 'chains' to produce a self-locking mechanism, a manoeuvring of strained contradictions into self-binding self-cancellations: the end-term is a complex *impasse* internally structured by its own dynamics and therefore with a kind of *stasis*, a 'moment' of truce, a perversely satisfactory stalemate. The 'end' of writing, the completion of the work, comes when any re-entry into the process of the text—by (re-) reading it—leads to that *impasse*.

At that point, the text can be left alone, abandoned as self-supporting, as self-constrainted, but awaiting another — a reader who will set its movements in motion once more, only for them, and the reader, to arrive once more at their achieved impasse. Neither the writing nor the reading of the text can arrive at a 'resolution' of the contradictions which are displaced and condensed in the process of reading and writing, and re-reading and re-writing: those operations may, eventually, allow but a temporary truce in the continual struggle with those contradictions.

The specific impasse of *The Fall* can be likened to that of a judge judging himself to be unjust according to laws which he judges to be unjust and which disqualify him from judging by them —an endless vicious circle which may be the deepest in hell.

But the specific operations of this text perhaps suggest a general procedure which characterises and constitutes the process of any work which provides 'aesthetic' satisfaction or contentment, and gives some hint as to why some art-work is 'better', more satisfying, than other (art-)work.

Think of the well-known, if apocryphal, Oxford philosophy examination paper: the candidate opens the envelope and finds a single sheet of paper, on which is written:

> Is the sentence on the back of this paper
> a question?

The candidate turns over the sheet of paper; the reverse side is blank. Faced with that, what does one do, what does one write? The possibilities are endless. But what guides in the search for the 'right' response? Basically, it's the need not to 'answer' the 'question' but rather to 'block' the problem being confronted, to write something which will turn that 'question' back upon itself, either cancelling it out or giving back the problem to the examiner. The candidate might write: 'If this is an answer.' If the examiner responds with 'No, it isn't', the logic of that 'if' concludes that the non-existent sentence was not a question—which is a kind of answer. What, though, would be the 'best' 'answer', the most appropriate, the most satisfying response—at least for the examinee? We would, as examinees and perhaps as examiners, 'judge' between different possible responses in terms of the degree to which they 'constrainted' the original move in this 'exchange' between examinee and examiner, between also the front and back of this sheet of paper. I think I might most happily, and securely, leave the examination-hall ('finish' the paper), if I were to turn the sheet of paper over and write on the 'other' side:

> Is the sentence on the reverse of this paper
> a question?

The 'necessity' for a 'truce', the need to arrive at constraintment in writing, may arise from a more or less specific crisis or contradiction, for the writer in the first instance. In Camus's case perhaps that contradiction is legible in his pronouncements during the 1950S on Algeria:[18]

> 'You must choose your side,' cry the haters. Oh I have chosen it! I have chosen my country. I have chosen the

---

[18] Quoted by O'Brien, *Camus*, p.72, p. 75.

> Algeria of justice in which French and Arabs will associate freely.
>
> I have always condemned terror. I must also condemn a terrorism which operates blindly, in the streets of Algeria for example, and which one day may strike my mother or my family. I believe in justice but I will defend my mother before justice.

In January 1956, the year of the publication of *La Chute*, Camus went to Algeria to propose the one concrete idea he had: a 'truce for civilians'.

The specific contradictions of a white French Algerian in 1956-7 are an instance of that pervasive contradiction that turns support for 'justice' into acquiescence in 'injustice' when we ourselves become the targets in a 'just war' of liberation—in such a situation, faced with that problem, we would all prefer to be civilians. But though a constraintment of those contradictions may temporarily be found in the art-work—in the work of writing and of reading—there is no truce possible outside of that work: at most, writing or reading a work of art may allow us, for a few privileged moments, to 'work through' some of the permutations of those contradictions which already shape our 'damaged lives' (to use Adorno's phrase from *Minima Moralia*), may even allow us access to an 'understanding' of them, in the process of which we may arrive at the peculiar satisfaction of 'inhabiting' the world which would be constituted by their permanent, static, self-constraintment: a steady state world from which the actual movements of history have been expelled. There, perhaps, lies literature's subtlest attraction and temptation. In the end, however, those contradictions are, necessarily, worked through according to another logic, with quite other rules and procedures, and within that logic, the logic of history, there can be no truce at all. Always, with a shock, the dreamer has to awake—to find that the war is still continuing.

*

www.ingramcontent.com/pod-product-compliance
Lightning Source LLC
Chambersburg PA
CBHW050948050726
47592CB00007B/2487